COPING

IN

An Interfaith

Family

Gwen K. Packard

THE ROSEN PUBLISHING GROUP, INC./NEW YORK

Published in 1993 by The Rosen Publishing Group, Inc.
29 East 21st Street, New York, NY 10010

Copyright 1993 by Gwen K. Packard

First Edition

Packard, Gwen K.
　　Coping in an interfaith family / Gwen K. Packard.
　　　　p.　　cm.
　　Includes bibliographical references and index.
　　Summary: Discusses the effects of living in an interfaith family,
with an emphasis on the strengthening of spirituality, the
promotion of accepting differences, and other positive aspects.
　　ISBN 0-8239-1452-6
　　1. Interfaith marriage—United States—Juvenile literature.
2. Interfaith families—United States—Juvenile literature.
3. Family—United States—Religious life—Juvenile literture.
[1. Interfaith marriage. 2. Interfaith families.] I. Title.
HQ1031.P33 1993
306.84'3—dc20　　　　　　　　　　　　　　　　92-39454
　　　　　　　　　　　　　　　　　　　　　　　　　　CIP
　　　　　　　　　　　　　　　　　　　　　　　　　　AP

Manufactured in the United States of America

To Don, with love and gratitude

Acknowledgments

I want to thank the members of the clergy, social workers, librarians, and other professionals who gave of their time and expertise to answer my questions and help gather information for this book. A very special thanks to the many interfaith families who shared their experiences and opinions with me.

The names of the family members have been changed to protect their privacy. The names of members of the clergy, social workers, and other professionals have not been changed; they are quoted throughout the book.

ABOUT THE AUTHOR ◇

As a free-lance writer of fiction and nonfiction for adults and children, Gwen Packard is interested in young adult and children's issues, education, and health care. While doing research for a magazine article on interfaith families, she discovered that there was very little material for teenagers on the subject. This book is intended to help fill that gap.

Ms. Packard earned a Bachelor of Science in Education from Northwestern University and a Master of Arts in Library Science from Rosary College. Before becoming a writer, she was a children's librarian for almost fourteen years. She is a member of the Society of Children's Book Writers, the Children's Reading Round Table of Chicago, and the Off Campus Writers Workshop.

When she finds the time, Gwen Packard likes to play the viola and work on arts and crafts. She lives with her husband, Don, in a suburb of Chicago; and she has two grown children, Susan and Warren.

Contents

Introduction   vii

1   Promises and Policies: Intermarriage in Today's World   1

2   "Love Will Fix Everything"   14

3   A Part of Life: Religion in the Home   33

4   Whose Religion Is It, Anyway?   45

5   Building Relationships   63

6   The December Dilemma and Other Holidays   75

7   Sharing Religious Experiences   90

8   A Personal Decision: Conversion   107

9   Changes and Choices: Interfaith Teens   121

10   Aid and Comfort to the Interfaith Family   138

11   "It Works for Us"   150

Glossary   166

Appendix   169

For Further Reading   176

Index   179

Introduction

"An interfaith family is special because the children get the best of both worlds, culturally and genetically."
—Yosef, father of a Muslim-Christian family

"Growing up in an interfaith family is not necessarily special, but it's different. It's different from other families; where they only have one religion, I have two."
—Stacey, age eighteen,
growing up in a Protestant-Jewish family

"We are simply two people of two religions trying to create a family."
—Maureen, mother of a Catholic-Jewish family

"I think there's a way to solve this whole issue, but we haven't found it yet."
—Claudia, mother of a Protestant-Catholic family

"We will be married thirty-one years, and religion was never, ever a problem."
—Roslyn, mother of a Hindu-Jewish family

"We believe in this family, and we believe in what we teach each other."
—Josh, age fifteen,
growing up in a Catholic-Jewish family

In today's world, interfaith families are a fact of life. Official religious policies on intermarriage are being modified, attitudes are changing, and the number of interfaith families is increasing. That means an increase in the probability that you are growing up in an interfaith family or will be involved in an interfaith relationship.

Whether an interfaith family, or a family where both parents are of the same religion, every family is different. This book illustrates how some interfaith families live, how they work out some of the problems they encounter, and what they consider to be the benefits and disadvantages of living in an interfaith family. The topics covered include the interfaith couple, establishing religion in the home, the religious identity of the children, getting along with family and friends, holiday celebrations and special events, conversion, the special concerns of interfaith teens, and support groups for interfaith families.

As a teenager, you may not yet be thinking about marriage and children. By covering these topics, however, *Coping in an Interfaith Family* tries to give you a complete picture of interfaith families, so you can see the issues from all sides. If you are living in an interfaith family, or if you have a friend who lives in one, this book will show you what is special about living and coping in it.

CHAPTER ◇ 1

Promises and Policies: Intermarriage in Today's World

L
aura, Elaine, and Jenny stood together on the corner waiting for the high school bus. It was early April, with a hint of spring in the air. Elaine frowned as she looked at her assignment notebook. "I'm going to have to do this math assignment before Sunday," she said. "Sunday is Easter, and I'll be busy all day. First there's church services, and then we go to my grandmother's for a big Easter dinner."

"I'll be busy, too," Laura said. "Sunday is the first night of Passover. I have to help Mom get ready. I think a zillion relatives are coming for the seder."

1

The two girls looked at Jenny. "What are you doing Sunday?" Laura asked.

"I'm not sure," Jenny replied. "We always have a seder with my dad's family. But my mom's family wants us to come for their Easter dinner. It's a tradition, too."

"So, what will you do?" Elaine asked.

"Mom and Dad will decide," Jenny answered. "Passover and Easter usually don't fall on the same day. This year we will have to compromise."

"It must be hard to cope when your parents have two different religions," Elaine said.

Jenny smiled. "Sometimes it's hard, but most of the time it's nice," she said. "Besides, I get two holidays instead of one!"

Jenny is growing up in an interfaith family, a situation that is becoming more common every day. Like all families, interfaith families come in a variety of shapes and sizes. Although Catholic-Protestant and Christian-Jewish families are the most common combinations, many other religious combinations can and do exist. A family may be Islamic-Christian, Jewish-Hindu, Catholic-Orthodox, Buddhist-Christian, Hindu-Sikh. The family may decide to practice the religion of only one parent, a combination of both religions, a different religion from that of either parent, or no religion at all.

Basically, an interfaith marriage is a "union between two people of different faith communities," according to Rabbi Vernon Kurtz. Interfaith marriage has different names: intermarriage, mixed marriage, interreligious marriage, or Jewish-Gentile marriage. A Catholic-Protestant family may be called ecumenical, interdenominational, interchurch, or interconfessional.

Most of the experts interested in the religious or family aspects of the subject agree that the number of inter-marriages in the United States is increasing rapidly. The exact number must be estimated from small samples or personal experience. Questions on religious identity do not appear in the United States Census. No current government statistics show the exact number of inter-marriages. Surveys have been conducted by private religious groups such as the United States Catholic Conference and the Council of Jewish Federations. Dr. Man Keung Ho, a professor of social work and expert in marriage and family therapy, estimates that one out of every three marriages in the United States is an intermarriage.

The percentage of Catholics marrying non-Catholics has been rising for many years. A 1981 study conducted by the United States Catholic Conference estimated the rate of Catholic intermarriage at forty percent. The figures differ from one region of the country to another. In the South, for instance, where the Catholic population is smaller, mixed marriage figures may go as high as seventy-five percent.

Frank Hannigan, Director for Family Ministries of the Catholic Archdiocese of Chicago, says that there are about 13,000 marriages in the archdiocese annually. Of these, about twenty-two percent are interfaith, Catholics marrying non-Catholics. There are twenty-two marriage preparation centers in the Chicago area. Some have few interfaith couples; others have as many as seventy percent.

In European nations where a high percentage of the population belongs to Eastern Orthodox sects such as Greek Orthodox or Russian Orthodox, intermarriage is rare. In the United States where membership is low, however, about seventy-five percent of Eastern Orthodox marriages are mixed, going as high as ninety percent in some areas of the country.

Until 1960, only about five percent of American Jews who married chose spouses from other religions. By the mid-1960s, the number had risen to more than fifteen percent; in the 1980s, as high as fifty percent. In 1992, the rate of Jews intermarrying ranged from thirty-five to eighty percent, depending on the area of the country. It is predicted that by the year 2000, half of the students in Reform Jewish religious schools will have one parent who was not born Jewish.

Some communities may have no interfaith families, whereas in others the incidence may be very high. A woman who is raising her children in an interfaith home asked, "Isn't everyone in this town intermarried?" Another said that ninety percent of her friends were interfaith couples.

Intermarriage is not a new phenomenon. It has been recorded in the Bible. In many verses of the Old Testament, the Israelites are warned not to marry the sons or daughters of another people, calling it evil and a transgression against God. "King Solomon loved many strange women . . ." and was warned not to marry them, ". . . for surely they will turn away your heart after their gods. . . ." (I Kings 11:1–2) Other Biblical passages, such as the story of Ruth, show a more positive view of inter-marriage, loyalty, and conversion.

Many of the world's religions have laws governing inter-marriage. The laws of some religious groups have remained the same over centuries. Other groups, recognizing that intermarriage is a fact of life in today's world, have made modifications to accommodate changing attitudes and life-styles. Some religions are now more tolerant of interfaith marriage than they were in the past.

Fifty years ago, Catholicism formally discouraged marriage with non-Catholics. The official position of the Church has changed considerably in the twentieth century, especially since Vatican Council II in 1965. Before that year, the Code of Canon Law required the non-Catholic partner to make certain promises, including a pledge that the couple's children would be baptized and educated in the Catholic faith. Weddings had to be performed outside the Church, but the vows were to be said before a Catholic priest, not a minister or rabbi. Catholic clergy were instructed to dissuade their parishioners from mixed marriage to the best of their ability.

Matrimonii Sacramentum, written in 1966 to modify the law on mixed marriages, eliminated the law prohibiting a Catholic from being married by a non-Catholic minister. It also changed the required promise of the non-Catholic to baptize and educate the children in the Catholic faith to an invitation to promise not to prevent the Catholic spouse from doing so.

Karen, a Jewish woman who married a Catholic man, says, "I signed a statement that I would not stand in Nick's way if he wanted to raise our children Catholic. It didn't say that we must raise our children Catholic, but that I wouldn't stand in his way. I felt okay about that."

A Catholic must receive permission, or dispensation, to marry a non-Catholic Christian. If a Catholic marries a non-Catholic outside of the Church, they also must have dispensation, or the marriage will not be recognized. Dispensation—the exemption of a Catholic from a church law or obligation—used to be discouraged but now is routine. The Catholic still promises to remain faithful to the tenets of Catholicism and "to do all in their power to see that their children are raised as Catholics," says Father Michael Place, Research Theologian to the Curia, Archdiocese of Chicago. "The non-Catholic partner is made aware of these promises."

"Ninety-nine percent of the time, dispensation is granted," says Father Place. The rare exception would be if the local priest decides that the Catholic really does not believe in the Catholic faith and is only marrying in the faith to please a parent or for some superstitious reason. "So why go through all this fuss, if you don't believe anyway?" he asks.

"The Catholic Church no longer specifically discourages intermarriage," Father Place continues. "But they do want couples to be aware of the significance of their choice for the family. If both partners have a strong faith, that will be a source of tension in the marriage. The interfaith couple must begin early to decide how to integrate their faiths into a healthy marriage."

With the new policies, it is also possible for a Catholic to obtain permission to be married in the church of the non-Catholic partner. Eric, a Catholic, had to get dispensation to marry Claudia in her Protestant church. "Dispensation is an application process," Eric explains. "In essence the church is saying, 'If you marry someone who is not Catholic, you don't know what you're doing.' They want to be sure that you're marrying a good person. They check that person's record of baptism.

"My priest was not disturbed when I decided to be married in the Congregational church. These days, mixed marriages are performed as much by the Catholic Church as the Protestant. It happens so often, it's not a big deal."

Elena, who is Catholic, and Ray, who is Jewish, were

married at the time of Vatican II. They have firsthand knowledge of the changes in policy created by the Council. "Speaking for Ray, he never felt anything but good with those priests," Elena says. "If it had been five years earlier, I think we couldn't have gotten by."

"We were right in Vatican II, right at the moment in 1967," Ray says. "Council met in 1965, and all these changes were being effected as we went through it. In the few talks I had with the parish priest, there was never a demand for conversion or anything at all."

"Ray had to go through six hours of instruction. That was the rule of the Church before we were married," Elena says. "The non-Catholic spouse was to sign a paper promising not to practice birth control and to raise the children Catholic. It was all changing. Within months you didn't have to do that. But at that time the rule still was that the non-Catholic had to sign."

"When that moment came, I just didn't sign," Ray says. "There was never any pressure on me."

Catholic priest Father Ron Scarlatta recalls events in his life that reflect the changes in the Catholic Church in relation to intermarriage. "When I was five years old, my cousin married a Jewish woman, and the wedding took place in the rectory, the priest's house. The next family interfaith wedding was in the church, but 'outside the rail,' not in the sanctuary. The next was in the sanctuary, but it was a wedding ceremony, not a mass. Today, the wedding may be held outside the church, or with a non-Catholic minister, and still be recognized."

Unlike the laws governing intermarriage in the Catholic Church, those of the Eastern Orthodox Church have not been modified recently. According to Greek Orthodox priest Father Mark Elliott, the Orthodox Church allows mixed marriage between an Orthodox in good standing in the church with a non-Orthodox Trinitarian Christian, a Catholic, or a Protestant. The marriage must be performed in the Oxthodox church by an Orthodox priest. An Orthodox priest would not go to a Catholic church to perform a marriage. However, a Catholic priest could attend an Orthodox wedding and offer a blessing after the marriage ceremony.

"An Orthodox priest cannot celebrate the marriage of an Orthodox to a non-Christian," Father Mark says. "There could be a secular marriage, but then the Orthodox partner would no longer be in good standing with the church and would not be able to receive the sacraments."

Changes in the Catholic Church have had an impact on Protestants. "Since Vatican II, there is more dialog between Protestants and Catholics," says Presbyterian minister Donna Gray. "People are seriously looking at each other's faith. It is a dramatic change. Protestant ministers are now invited to the Catholic church to participate in mixed marriages."

Although there is no single overall policy on intermarriage, Protestant ministers can and do perform interfaith marriages. "Policies vary from denomination to denomination," the minister explains. "In the Congregational church, the congregation decides. In the Presbyterian Church, the church provides position papers that are advisory, not dictum. It is up to each minister to decide. Some are comfortable officiating at a mixed marriage, some are not."

She and her husband and copastor, Carl Gray, have officiated at interfaith marriages. "We have been to Jewish weddings, where the ceremony was more Jewish. And we have had Christian-Jewish weddings in the church where the emphasis is more Christian," Donna Gray says.

Mitch is a Protestant married to Debbie, who is Jewish. His parents are leaders in their church. "Protestant church policy on interfaith marriage is not written," Mitch says. "But most churches would like to see marriages within the faith. Then there would be no problem; children are born into the faith, and the congregation would get new members all the time. Recently a rabbi said that Jews should marry Jews. He made a big issue out of it, and he stated it out in the open. I think all religious groups feel the same way, whether they state it or not."

The official position of Orthodox Judaism on intermarriage is "absolutely negative," according to Gedalia Dov Schwartz, Chief Presiding Judge of the Rabbinical Court of the Chicago Rabbinical Council. "There cannot be any intermarriage. If people convert to Judaism, they may marry only after conversion. A religious Orthodox person will not intermarry. Someone from an Orthodox home may intermarry, but the marriage will not be recognized by Orthodox Judaism." To prevent intermarriage, the Rabbinical Council constantly preaches and teaches what they see as the consequences of intermarriage: children lost to Judaism, adults lost to Judaism.

In the musical *Fiddler on the Roof*, Chava, the third daughter of the Jewish peasant Tevye, is considered "dead" by her family when she marries a non-Jewish Russian. Although the original story was written decades ago, the attitude of Orthodox Jews toward intermarriage has changed little.

As with Orthodox Judaism, Conservative Judaism is opposed to intermarriage. A Conservative rabbi may not officiate at the wedding of an interfaith couple and may not even be present at the ceremony. According to an official of Conservative Judaism, "Mixed marriage is regarded as a civil marriage. It is not recognized as a Jewish marriage by Conservative Jews."

"To Jews, intermarriage is not just a religious issue, it is a peoplehood issue," says Conservative Rabbi Vernon Kurtz. "Nobody can prevent intermarriage in this society. Instead of just reacting to intermarriage, we are working with teens and college students before they marry, giving information, and counseling couples about the problems involved in intermarriage. Marriage is difficult as it is. Interfaith marriage can create even more disagreements."

When young adults do intermarry, the rabbi may work with the couple's parents, not to condone the relationship, but to help the parents with the reality. "We don't want to reject the couple, although some may feel rejected," Rabbi Kurtz says. "We must maintain high and consistent standards. Conservative rabbis are sending a mixed message—not on intermarriage, because that is not condoned—but on the relationship. They do not condone the relationship, but they do not reject the couple. In Conservative Judaism, there is now more effort neither to close the door nor to condemn the couple."

In 1909, the Central Conference of American Rabbis (CCAR), composed of rabbis from the Reform Jewish movement, adopted the stand that ". . . mixed marriage is contrary to the Jewish tradition and should be discouraged." In 1973, the group expanded this declaration by resolving ". . . its opposition to participation by its members in any ceremony which solemnizes a mixed marriage." Although some Reform rabbis will officiate at an interfaith wedding, a majority of members of CCAR have always voted against officiating at mixed marriages.

"Officiation at a mixed marriage is a difficult issue that

rabbis struggle with daily," says Reform Rabbi Herbert Bronstein. "There is no issue that has been so agonizing as the issue of officiation." He spends more time talking with couples for whom he cannot officiate than with those he can. "The presence of a rabbi does not make it a Jewish wedding," Rabbi Bronstein explains. The rabbi represents the Jewish community and tradition. The couple marry each other "within the covenant of God and the Jewish people," which assumes that both partners are Jewish and that the covenant will be continued.

Islam prohibits marrying outside the faith, with two exceptions: A Muslim man may marry a Christian or a Jewish woman, called Women of the Book. The woman must have good morals. The couple must raise their children as Muslims. Although different Islamic sects may impose more restrictions, it is unlawful for a Muslim man to marry a polytheist (someone who worships more than one god) or an atheist, unless she becomes a Muslim.

A Muslim woman may marry only a man who is a Muslim. If a Muslim woman marries a non-Muslim, he is given a grace period of about two months to study and accept Islam. Otherwise, the marriage is not recognized.

Buddhism has no official policy on intermarriage. Many mixed marriages are performed in Buddhist temples. In the view of many Buddhists, marriage is a private, civil event, not a religious rite.

In traditional Hinduism, intermarriage is unacceptable. There is little commingling even among the various castes (hereditary classes) of the religion, let alone with other religions. The four castes do not associate socially or intermarry.

As the official policies of many religions are becoming more liberal, attitudes are also changing. In the past, intermarriage may have been viewed as an abnormality or even a disgrace. A recent study by the United States Catholic Conference indicates a "trend toward greater acceptance" of intermarriage. In fact, this greater acceptance is one of the reasons intermarriage is increasing.

The 1990 National Jewish Population Survey sponsored by the Council of Jewish Federations found little opposition to intermarriage among survey participants. Over seventy-five percent of the respondents said they would either support or accept the intermarriage of their children. The study concluded that the acceptance of intermarriage coincides with its rapid rise in recent years.

Reform Rabbi Stephen Hart, who works with many interfaith couples, says, "We need to respond to the phenomenon of intermarriage, but not as we did in the past, ripping our clothes and talking about how awful it is, or turning our heads, but in very concrete ways to respond to it."

In 1955, Vivian and Ralph dated for several months before Ralph asked her to marry him. Ralph was a Protestant who had little interest in religion. Vivian was a Catholic. Because of pressure from her parents, as well as her own beliefs, Vivian insisted that Ralph become a Catholic before they married. Ralph converted and became a devout Catholic. Thirty years later, their son, Nick, wanted to marry Karen, a Jewish woman. Both Vivian and Ralph accepted Nick's decision; neither insisted that Karen become a Catholic. Over thirty years, attitudes had changed.

Greta grew up in an interfaith family. Her own two sons were raised in a Jewish household. Each son married a non-Jewish woman. Greta can see the contrast in attitudes between the generations. "It was so difficult for my parents," she says. "I remember how terrible it was for them. We were always the outsiders. Today, interfaith families are accepted, at least on the surface."

"I remember when I was a teenager," Fran recalls. "If the children of my mother's friends intermarried—and it didn't happen very often—my mother talked about it as if it were a funeral, not a wedding. Today, almost all the children of my own friends are intermarried, and the weddings are the happy occasions they should be."

CHAPTER 2

"Love Will Fix Everything"

When Lisa married Jeb, the wedding was a conglomeration of religious and cultural traditions. Lisa's mother is Jewish, and her father is Hindu. Jeb's family is Jain, another Eastern religion. "We had a Hindu ceremony in English with a female priest and a religious Hindu teacher," Lisa says. "My Jewish grandfather gave the blessing over the challah, the braided bread, which is a Jewish tradition. Jeb's uncle gave a blessing from the Sikhs, yet another Eastern religion. A Catholic priest gave a toast, and there were Jain prayers. The music was from many different traditions, too. It was truly an ecumenical wedding."

An interfaith family starts with an interfaith couple. There are many reasons that a young man and young woman of different faiths date each other and then decide to get married. In today's mobile society, young people often leave their religious and ethnic communities to attend college or find a job. They have more opportunities to meet people of different cultural backgrounds and faiths. By the same token, they may not have as many chances to meet people of the same religion.

"I grew up near Washington, D.C.," says Melanie, a Chinese woman who was brought up a Baptist and married a Jew. "Washington is a very diverse, open environment. A lot of my friends were Jewish. I socialized with them. I attended bar mitzvahs. When I took philosophy in college, it was the first time I had studied religion. From my Chinese perspective, I viewed the Judaic and Christian religions as one. As Western religions, they have a lot in common."

Attitudes toward interfaith dating and intermarriage are more liberal than they were thirty or more years ago. There is more religious tolerance. Some religious institutions have relaxed or modified their restrictions on intermarriage. Some people actually feel more comfortable with people from a different culture. Others may be rebelling against their background. Many of today's young people have less interest in religion than their parents did.

Or it may simply be a case of two people meeting, falling in love, and deciding to marry, without regard for religion.

The young people involved in interfaith relationships come from many backgrounds, with varying degrees of religious observance. Some grew up in homes where religion was an important part of family life. For others, religion was unimportant or even absent from the home.

Many young people grow up in what they consider to be a religious environment. Their parents are active in the church, synagogue, mosque, or temple. Often, these young people also participate in religious activities. The parents probably assume that the children will marry someone of the same faith and encourage that type of relationship. However, it does not always work out that way.

"Everyone in my family is Catholic," Elena says. "I was educated in Catholic schools from first grade through college. I came from a large family. All six of us went to Catholic schools, and all my nieces and nephews went to Catholic schools up to college. I certainly never dreamed I would be in an interfaith marriage." But Elena did marry Ray, a Jew.

Karen was brought up in a conservative Jewish household with many traditional family observances. She went to Hebrew school, and as a teenager she was active in the synagogue youth group. In college, Karen joined Hillel, an organization for Jewish students.

When Karen was eighteen and a freshman in college, she dated and agreed to marry a Jewish man who intended to become a rabbi. "There was the announcement in my father's home. Everybody was crying and happy," Karen says. "But it didn't work out. After that I never dated anybody Jewish. I never met anybody Jewish that I liked." Karen met Nick in college, where they both worked on the radio station. Nick's family were practicing Catholics. His mother and father still go to church every week. Nick liked the Catholic religion. He was an altar boy, and he was active in the church until he was a teenager.

Both Claudia, a Protestant, and Eric, a Catholic, had strong religious backgrounds before they met. "I went to the Congregational Sunday School regularly, and I was in the church choir and youth organization," Claudia says. Eric attended Catholic grade school and high school. "They were all-boy Jesuit schools. School, church, sports, everything was church-related," Eric says. "Religion was a regular part of the program. We had religion class every day. But did I think about marrying a Catholic woman? It wasn't high on my list."

Melanie and her husband, Glenn, do not have strong religious backgrounds. Melanie is Chinese. Born in Taiwan, she was christened by Baptist missionaries as a child and attended Baptist church. "I am a philosopher," Melanie says. "I follow no particular religion, but I believe in God and the spiritual part of religion." Glenn is Jewish. "I grew up in a secular household where religion wasn't an issue," he says. "My brother is active in the Jewish community, but my sister married a Catholic."

Some of the young adults who intermarry also grew up in interfaith homes. Their mothers and fathers were of different religions. Sometimes even brothers and sisters had different faiths. Children from interfaith homes are more likely to intermarry than those who come from single-faith families. If an older brother or sister—or uncle or cousin—has intermarried, it is easier for a younger sibling to do so.

Cheryl is from an interfaith family. Her mother is Jewish, and her father is Christian. She was brought up as "what my mother calls a secular Jew." She attended Sunday School at a school that did not teach about God and never mentioned the synagogue, but taught history, tradition, and customs. "I grew up with a Christmas tree, and we used to go to my father's parents' house for Christmas dinner. I had a cousin who sang in the church choir."

Sandy's father was Jewish and her mother was Catholic. Sandy was brought up Catholic and married a Jew. "I was baptized a Catholic and I went to Catholic school," she says. "But by the time I was an adolescent, I much more identified with my father. So I decided I wasn't Catholic anymore; I was going to be Jewish. I didn't specifically look for someone Jewish to marry. I thought it was a good fit because Dad was Jewish and my college was predominantly Jewish."

The religious makeup of the community can influence religious choices. If it is an environment of diverse cultures, children have a greater opportunity to meet people from different religions. On the other hand, some children do not have the opportunity to meet others of the same religion. Renee was brought up Jewish in a city where only two percent of the population was Jewish. "I grew up in a Christian world," Renee says. In another case, Omir and Daud lived in a town where theirs was the only Islamic family.

When young people from Eastern religions, such as Buddhism and Hinduism, live in a Western society like the United States, their values can be quite different from their parents' values. In India, Hindus do not intermarry, even between sects or castes of the same religion. In the United States, where intermarriage is more acceptable, about half the young Hindus intermarry.

"It's the dilemma of the twenty-first century," a Christian minister says. "We want our children to live in an open secular society, yet marry within the faith. We can't put blinders on them."

Many young adults assume that they will marry someone of the same faith. They do not approve of intermarriage, believing that there are many problems associated with it. Yet, once they fall in love with someone of a different religion and decide to marry that person, their differences are no longer a major factor in the relationship.

"I am a member of the Congregational Church. That's about as far on the spectrum as you can get from Catholicism," Claudia says. "Eric and I assumed there would be problems. The first problem was that neither of us wanted to change our religion. But we talked about it, and we decided that we could live with it." "We decided that, because we were both of the Christian faith, it wouldn't be a real big problem," Eric adds. "It happens so often, it's not a big deal."

Before she met Ray, Elena believed that people should marry within their faith. "I felt pretty strongly that a Catholic should marry a Catholic," she says. "I thought that life was hard enough. A couple needs the unity of faith to strengthen their marriage."

Marilyn preferred not to marry someone non-Jewish. "I knew it would create difficulties. But at the same time, it wasn't the overriding issue." Larry was Christian, but he didn't care at all about religion. "It wasn't as though we had to worry about practicing two religions," Marilyn continues. "He was a nonpracticing Christian. I was almost nonpracticing at the time, but I felt this strong Jewish identity."

In an effort to avoid problems, Debbie, who is Jewish, explained her feelings to Mitch, a Protestant, before they were married. "I said I didn't think I could live near his parents, because they are extremely religious. They go to church three days a week or more. They are high priests in the church; for them, everything is church. I said, there's no way I could do that. If he planned to marry me, I wanted to raise my kids Jewish. Not that I even like to go to the synagogue, but I couldn't see making my kids go to church three or four days a week. As much as I loved

him, I didn't love him so much that I wanted to change
my entire life to be like his family. So it was his choice all
the way."

When Yosef, a Muslim from Pakistan, came to the
United States, he did not intend to intermarry. He did
keep an open mind, however, and did not restrict his
choice to Muslim women. He decided he would marry
the person he liked. That turned out to be Elizabeth, a
Protestant who converted to Islam.

Helen, a Japanese-American born a Christian, married
Robert, a Japanese-American Buddhist. Helen was not
concerned about the differences in religions, but believed
a person should marry someone of the same nationality or
culture. "What the person is like is the important thing,"
Helen says, "not the religion."

Early in the interfaith couple's relationship, their parents
may not be happy about the idea of their child's marrying
someone of a different faith. Later, most parents accept
the situation, and many become supportive of the couple.
Many parents support the decision because they do
not want to lose their children. Others are supportive
from the very beginning. A rabbi says that the parents'
reactions may range from anger and guilt to denial to
hope. They may silently accept the marriage or ask many
questions to be sure the young couple have worked out
problems in their own minds.

Jeanette is a Jewish woman whose son married a
Japanese Shinto woman and whose daughter married a
Protestant Christian. Her attitude is shared by many
parents of young adults who have intermarried. She says,
"Of course I would have preferred that my children had

married into solidly Jewish families, but I have no complaints. I am very much attached to my daughter-in-law and son-in-law."

Because Jews are a small minority of the world's population, many Jewish parents view intermarriage as a threat to the religion's survival. One father said that intermarriage would be the end of the Jewish people. When his daughter decided to intermarry, he was not happy. Another Jewish father said, "You are only making it hard on yourself by marrying someone of a different faith."

Glenn's parents considered intermarriage "disastrous" for the Jewish people. They wanted him to marry a Jew. "I didn't understand why it was such an exclusive club," Glenn says.

Marilyn's mother shared her daughter's viewpoint. Marilyn says, "She felt it would be easier, more practical, to marry someone Jewish; but other things were more important. She was very supportive. My sister had married a non-Jew. That sort of broke the ice. My parents always had a preference that we marry someone Jewish. But they were not like the parents of some friends of ours who wouldn't even let a man in the house if he wasn't Jewish. We knew what they preferred, but we always felt that they would be very accepting of what we did."

For some parents, it takes time to accept the interfaith marriage of their child. A couple may be married for several years before a parent stops being concerned about the religious differences. Although Karen's mother was supportive, her father took a long time to accept his daughter's interfaith marriage. Karen and Nick announced their engagement in December and planned to be married the following September. It was July before Karen's father agreed to come to the wedding. "It was a long time. He was the one who almost forced the religious issue," Karen says.

"I knew that her father was not keen on our relationship," Nick comments. "But I just decided that that was his loss."

In Nick's family, it was not a problem that Karen was Jewish. "It was no more than an off-hand comment," Nick says. "'Is she Catholic?' 'No, she's Jewish.' That was it. It really was not important. It didn't matter."

Mitch's parents are leaders in their Protestant church. They had a positive reaction to Mitch's decision to marry Debbie, who is Jewish. "My parents feel that being Jewish is being one of the chosen," Mitch says. "I don't think too many people can say that with a straight face, but it works in with their religious philosophy."

Debbie's parents were also accepting. "I was raised where the emphasis was not, 'You must marry someone of your religion.' It was, 'Marry a good person, a kind person, someone who loves kids, someone who loves you and takes your view.' I don't think religion was a major factor. In fact, if I had brought home a jerk, it wouldn't have mattered what religion he was."

Some parents never accept the intermarriage of their child. William, from a Greek Orthodox background, was planning to marry Laura, a Jewish woman, but William was being rejected by his family. If the relationship continued, he would no longer be considered a part of his family. There was tremendous emotional pain for William and Laura, trying to work out their commitment to each other and at the same time work out the responses of the family.

"There are a variety of approaches to the situation," says Father Mark Elliott. "If the Orthodox partner's faith is strong, the other may convert; or they may call off the wedding. If the couple feel their love is stronger than their faith, they will get married. Parents must deal with the disappointment. They may feel they have failed as parents because their children are marrying outside the faith."

"In the Eastern Orthodox family, there can be a lot of pressure to marry within the faith," Father Mark says. "Sometimes there is even a problem marrying outside the ethnic group. It depends on the relationship of the parents and children in the family. For an immigrant family from a country where there is virtually only one religion, mixed marriage may seem like an impossibility. But, in America, it is reality."

Sandy, whose father is Jewish and mother is Catholic, was brought up a Catholic. She and Daniel, who was from an Orthodox Jewish family, were married as an interfaith couple by a rabbi in his office. None of Daniel's family attended the wedding. "It turned out to be a very small wedding," Sandy says. "A few good friends, my sister, and my father and stepmother were the only ones there. Everybody was so angry about it.

"My mother did not attend because she felt I was making the same mistake that she had. By that time my parents were already divorced. My mother thought, 'Oh no, she's doing just what I did.' My father thought it was fine. Religion wasn't what separated them, and religion wasn't the big issue in our house.

"It was a real conflict. Because my father is Jewish but not my mother, I was not considered Jewish by Daniel's family. When we were planning to get married, he would get these threatening letters from Israel, telling him that if he marries this woman who is not Jewish they will disown him."

Roslyn, a Jewish woman who married Lee, a Hindu, discovered cultural differences in the reactions to her marriage. "When we got married, nobody in India asked me about my religion," Roslyn says. "Everybody in this country asked me how we were going to raise our children. It's interesting how people focus."

Roslyn's daughter, Lisa, agrees. "The first time my in-laws asked me what I believed in was four months after our wedding. They never asked me before."

Sometimes, for the parents of an interfaith couple, religion becomes a coverup for other problems. Some parents feel a sense of loss, that they and their values are being rejected, or that they are losing control of their children. They may feel guilty that they did not raise their child right. If the young couple plan to move to a distant city after they are married, or if they are facing a difficult financial situation, parents may object to the marriage.

It is important for all couples—but especially interfaith couples—to communicate with their parents. Sheri and Steven dated for seven years and could not decide whether to get married. "We tried to guess how our parents would feel," Sheri says, "instead of sitting down and discussing it with them. You must communicate what you need, and what you are doing."

Roslyn recommends that young couples be open and honest with their parents. "Be straightforward. Don't give your parents any surprises. And definitely don't lie to them. The parents' hurt comes from within. Anybody you bring home is going to be a problem, because no parents are ready for their kid to have a significant other. Even if parents get angry, when they settle down they can discuss the real issues."

A father said, "Children sell parents short. They imagine

resistance that doesn't exist. Or they think parents will be more disruptive than supportive, which they are not."

One young woman said, "We worked things out to satisfy ourselves. And then, to please our parents, we had to work things out again."

Once an interfaith couple decide to get married, planning the wedding and finding a clergyman to officiate may present new problems. The wedding ceremony can take many forms, depending on the opinions of the young couple, their families, and their religious institutions. Instead of a clergyman, a judge or justice of the peace may conduct the ceremony. The couple may even be lucky enough to have a clergyman in the family. One couple, a Jewish woman and a non-Jewish man, were married by the groom's father, an Episcopal priest. In another case, the bride's sister-in-law was the minister for a Protestant-Catholic wedding. Many interfaith weddings do not take place in a house of worship, but in a hotel, club, or private home.

"We had to decide where to get married and how to get married," Eric says. "Claudia didn't want to be married in the Catholic church. So, we were married in the Congregational church with a Catholic priest co-officiating."

Eric's parents would have preferred that they be married in the Catholic church. Claudia's parents would have preferred that she marry a non-Catholic.

With the help of their minister, Claudia and Eric wrote their own wedding ceremony. "It was very unconventional," Claudia says. She also did not wear a veil.

"We were at a shower with Eric's family, and we were discussing wedding plans," Claudia explains. "When

Eric's aunts heard that I was not going to wear a wedding veil, they were extremely upset."

Eric chuckles. "When we were getting married, Claudia had to find at least twenty things to do differently."

Elena says, "We considered getting a rabbi to co-officiate, but we decided that would be artificial because we were going to have a Catholic priest, and it was a mass. So a young friend of mine who is Jewish sang from the Song of Songs. Some Jewish guests took offense at that. The organ played, and a guest told me the organ shouldn't be playing. Ray's family came, and I didn't realize it, but none of them had ever been in a Christian church before."

"What do you mean," Ray laughs, "*I* had never been in a Christian church before."

Because some of their friends had been married by a rabbi and a priest, Karen and Nick hoped to have a rabbi and a priest officiate at their wedding. They spoke to many rabbis. "All of them to a man said we were crazy and should not get married," Karen reports. "We were going against the essence of the wedding ceremony. I have mixed feelings, thinking back on it. The Catholics were accepting. I didn't want it to be the Jews who were unaccepting, although I understand why."

"Before we were married, I didn't understand how these rabbis could be so cold," Nick says. "Later, I discovered their motivation. Now I understand why rabbis won't officiate, but I still don't agree with them."

Karen and Nick were married by a federal judge. They wrote their own ceremony, and were married outdoors at twilight. 'We got very creative with the wedding ceremony," Karen says. "Everybody had a candle. It was very family-oriented. The judge said there was a religious atmosphere about the whole thing even though there was no priest or rabbi. Nick's mother was upset that we were not getting married in a church. But my father would have been very uncomfortable in a church."

As Karen and Nick discovered, many rabbis will not officiate at a mixed marriage, or impose strict guidelines before doing so. Reform Rabbi Stephen Hart says he will not officiate but may refer couples to rabbis who officiate with integrity and high standards. "These rabbis genuinely feel that this is in the best interest of the Jewish people. They have high standards, requiring the couple to maintain a Jewish home and raise their children Jewish. In this sense, I respect what these rabbis are doing. I respect them, but I disagree with them." Rabbi Hart also believes that premarital counseling for the interfaith couple is very important.

Rabbi Gary Gerson considers intermarriage a threat to the Jewish community. He will not officiate at a mixed marriage. But after a civil ceremony he will welcome a couple into the Jewish community, provided that they plan to have a Jewish home and raise their children Jewish. Rabbi Herbert Bronstein agrees. "I would prefer that an interfaith couple have a nonreligious ceremony," he says.

Although a majority of Reform rabbis do not officiate at mixed marriages, the number who do is increasing rapidly. In one region of the country alone, the number went from two to twenty in twenty years. Rabbi Arnold Kaiman believes that by officiating at a mixed marriage he is helping to create a meaningful extended family. "Neither partner in the marriage will lose their extended family," he says. "That would be a terrible start to a marriage." Rabbi Kaiman requires that the couple have a Jewish home but not shut out the non-Jewish partner. The couple must also have four hours of counseling with

the rabbi, and it is recommended that they take an Introduction to Judaism class.

Most of the rabbis who preside at intermarriages will
not co-officiate with a clergyman of another faith, nor will
they hold the wedding in a synagogue. Christian ministers
and priests are more likely to co-officiate and hold the
wedding in a church. One Catholic priest said he would
conduct the wedding of a Catholic woman and a Jewish
man *only* if the wedding was in the church. A Protestant-
Catholic wedding may be held in a Protestant church with
a Catholic priest co-officiating.

Melanie and Glenn first agreed to be married in a
Unitarian church. To them, religion was not an issue. But
Glenn's father wanted them to have a Jewish ceremony.
The hardest part was getting a rabbi. They finally found
a rabbi from the Hillel—an organization for Jewish
students—on a nearby college campus. To honor Melanie's
Chinese heritage and Glenn's Jewish background, they
had a Jewish ceremony in a hotel, followed by a reception
in a Chinese restaurant. "It was a wonderful rabbi and a
beautiful service," Melanie reports.

A Christian-Jewish ceremony may include a variety of
elements, such as vows from the Christian tradition and
stamping on the glass from the Jewish tradition. Passages
from both the Old and New Testaments of the Bible may
be read. A Christian-Jewish couple who were married by
a Methodist minister included the seven blessings that
are part of the traditional Jewish wedding. A Protestant
minister who married a Jewish woman had another
suggestion. "You can have a Jewish part to the ceremony
without a rabbi by including family members from the
Jewish side."

When both the bride and groom are Christian but of
different denominations, conflicts may still occur when

planning the wedding. One couple—a Ukrainian Orthodox man and a Polish Catholic woman—solved that problem by having two ceremonies. Since the man's parents insisted he be married in the Ukrainian Orthodox church, the first wedding was held there. The second wedding was in an Episcopal church.

When a Muslim man marries a non-Muslim, the couple may have two ceremonies, one Islamic and one Christian. Or they may be married at city hall. There is no clergy class in Islam. To be married, the couple need two Muslim witnesses.

When Michelle, a Buddhist, married Gary, a Christian, the wedding was held in an old traditional betsuin. "The sutra chanting made our college friends giggle," recalls Michelle. "But it was a cultural event for many people."

One of the questions an interfaith couple are most frequently asked is: "How will you raise the children?" Some of the couples know even before they are married how they plan to raise their children. One partner may insist that the children be raised in his or her religion and may even refuse to marry unless the other agrees. Others leave that decision until the children are born or even later.

When they were juniors in college, Patrick, a Protestant, proposed to Cheryl, who was brought up Jewish. Cheryl said no. She wanted children very much, and if she had children she wanted them raised as Jews. "You have to accept that or I can't marry you," Cheryl told Patrick.

Claudia, a Protestant who married a Catholic, felt it was important to raise her children as Christians. It was not so important whether they were raised Protestant or Catholic.

Before a couple are married, they may agree in theory how they will bring up their children. But once the children are born, both partners may feel differently. Roger, who is Christian, and Renee, who is Jewish, dated for seven years. The last couple of years before they were married, they had serious discussions about what it would mean if they had children. It was not even a question to Renee. "It was very important to me that I have a Jewish home and a Jewish family. What I didn't realize was that Roger had no idea what that meant, although he agreed to everything. Our religions are practiced so differently. When reality set in, he said, 'Wait a minute, did I agree to all this? Let's renegotiate.'"

As with many young couples, an interfaith couple's ideas and feelings can change many times during their relationship: from when they first meet, date, and fall in love, through planning the wedding, and after their marriage. Their religious background and the opinions of their parents influence their thinking.

Elizabeth was raised as a Protestant, in Iowa. When she met Yosef—a Muslim from Pakistan—in college, she was already considering converting to Islam. Yosef was influential and answered many of Elizabeth's questions. Elizabeth declared her acceptance of Islam minutes before the wedding ceremony.

While Roger and Renee were dating, they celebrated Christmas together and exchanged Christmas presents. "We were acting like a true interfaith couple," Roger says.

Renee does not agree. "I did not bring Judaism into any facet of our lives. I never told Roger when there was a Jewish holiday. As far as I'm concerned, I was totally in the Christian world."

When Roger and Renee got married, everything

changed. Renee wanted a Jewish home. The change was
very difficult for Roger. At the time he said, "Sure, that's
fine." But he didn't want to give up his Christian identity.
"We can't celebrate Christmas the way we did when we
were dating. We can't do a lot of the things we once did,
because Renee now feels different."

Every young couple planning to get married face a variety
of problems, such as gaining parental approval, planning
the wedding and finding a clergyman, and deciding how
to raise their children. For the interfaith couple, these
problems multiply.

Frank Hannigan, for the Catholic Church in one city,
works with couples about to be married, many of them
Catholic-Protestant or Catholic-Jewish couples. He says,
"Interfaith couples have the least realistic expectations of
marriage. They feel that love will fix everything. We don't
discourage intermarriage, but we do ask the couple to
take a realistic look at their relationship and look to the
future. If they are having serious problems now, problems
will only grow worse in the future. It is not up to us to say
don't get married. That is a decision the couple must
make."

Most clergy and social workers recommend that
engaged couples, whether interfaith or same-faith, receive
premarital counseling. Some religious groups require
it. What started in Frank Hannigan's diocese as Cana
days for marriage enrichment became pre-Cana classes
required of all couples being married in the Catholic
Church. "Over the years church leaders saw the wisdom
of properly preparing engaged couples for marriage,"
Hannigan explains. "In a way, all couples, even when

they are of the same religion, are interfaith. That's because their degree of faith will be different."

Greek Orthodox priest Father Mark Elliott recommends counseling for interfaith couples. "I speak with couples, not to prevent the mixed marriage, but to be sure that in their minds they are ready for the challenges of mixed marriage, and that they are informed of the consequences of the marriage." Premarital classes are required in some areas.

Protestant minister Donna Gray says that during premarital counseling through her church, couples are given a marriage inventory, which includes religion. "Religion is not an area that young couples talk about," she says. "Another topic on the inventory is in-laws. There may be pressure from in-laws on the religious issue."

Many interfaith couples acknowledge that intermarriage will present special problems. In most cases, they consider the problems surmountable and not as important as other factors.

Lynn and Richard anticipated problems, but it came to the point where the relationship was more important. "Problems are going to arise, but they can be dealt with."

Melanie and Glenn say they were "too much in love to fight about religion."

Marilyn and Larry agree. "Other factors are more important than religion. The fact that we love each other is the most important thing."

CHAPTER ◇ 3

A Part of Life:
Religion in the Home

A week after Easter, Laura, Elaine, and Jenny went to Jenny's house to plan the decorations for the Junior Class party that would be held in May. Elaine tapped the eraser end of her pencil against her cheek as she thought about arrangements. "The party will be on a Saturday night. Why don't we put up the decorations that morning?" she suggested.

Laura shook her head. "I can't come on a Saturday. It's *Shabbat*, the sabbath. I go to the synagogue in the morning. And I'm not supposed to work all day."

"Oh, lucky," teased Elaine. "What a great excuse. It's your day of rest."

Laura laughed with Elaine. "That's what it is. My dad's pretty strict about it."

"It's too bad religion has to mess up your life," Elaine said, more seriously.

"Religion doesn't really mess up your life," Jenny said.

"But it *is* a part of your life. I'm sure there are things that you can't do because of your religion, Elaine."

"Of course," Elaine answered. She remembered how she had to miss a friend's party because of a special mass.

Every Jewish home, every Protestant or Catholic home, every Islamic, Buddhist, or Hindu home has similar characteristics such as holidays celebrated and rituals observed. Yet every one of these homes is different, shaped by the personal beliefs of the parents, which are influenced by their own upbringing.

Same-faith homes, such as Laura Kaplan's Jewish home and Elaine Duffy's Catholic home, share certain characteristics. Often interfaith families, such as Jenny Adler's, follow only one religion and try to establish the home that way.

What does make a home Jewish, Catholic, Protestant, Islamic, Hindu, or Buddhist? Most families that follow a religion, no matter what that religion may be, have their special rites of passage and religious holidays, encourage religious education, and participate in prayer and ritual in the home as well as in the house of worship. Their religion can influence a family's way of life in the home and their personal values.

Rites of passage are rituals that mark an important event or milestone in life, such as birth, puberty, marriage, or death. Primitive or pagan societies also observed special rituals to commemorate these life-cycle events.

Although diverse in practice and belief, many of the world's religions have life-cycle rituals to mark infancy or young childhood. In Judaism, *b'rit milah* is the ritual for the circumcision and naming of an eight-day-old boy.

Muslims have a ceremony for the naming of a baby, as well as a ritual for the circumcision of a young boy. When a child is born to a Buddhist family, he is introduced into the church; a haircutting service is the formal entrance into Buddhism. Hindu rites of passage that occur in childhood include Namakarana, the naming ceremony, and Cudakarana, the first haircutting.

In the Christian family—Protestant, Catholic, and Orthodox—baptism is an important rite of passage. The Catholic and Orthodox churches and some Protestant churches baptize infants. Other denominations postpone baptism to adolescence or adulthood. In the Eastern Orthodox Church, along with baptism, an infant also receives chrismation (confirmation) and first communion, becoming a full member of the church.

Puberty rites, ceremonies marking the coming of age of an adolescent or young adult, are observed in almost all religions. These rituals mark the young person's acceptance into the community as an adult. *Bar mitzvah* for Jewish boys and *bat mitzvah* for Jewish girls occurs when they reach the age of thirteen. In the ceremony of confirmation, Jewish teens reconfirm their faith and affiliation with Judaism.

In churches that reserve baptism for adolescents and adults, it becomes the conscious choice of a mature person. Confirmation, another Christian rite that takes place during the teen years, is a reaffirmation of baptism. The Orthodox Church has no ritual or ceremony for adolescents.

In Hinduism, adolescent males participate in a rite of passage called Upanayana, an initiation viewed as a "second birth." In modern India, only males of the highest caste may participate in this rite.

In the home and the house of worship, people of every religion celebrate holidays based on seasonal and historical events. The major Christian holidays of Christmas, celebrating the birth of Jesus, and Easter, marking the resurrection of Christ, are familiar to most Americans. Major religious holidays for Jews include the High Holy Days: Rosh Hashanah, the New Year; and Yom Kippur, the Day of Atonement. The week-long festival of Passover, commemorating the liberation of Israel from Egypt, is also important. Although many non-Jews are familiar with the holiday of Hanukkah because it occurs close to Christmas, it is considered a minor holiday in the Jewish calendar.

Amir Ali, managing director of the Institute of Islamic Information and Education, explains that Muslims have two major religious holidays, or *eids*, when gifts of new clothes, toys, or money are given to children. Eid Al-Adha, the "Celebration of Sacrifice," commemorates Abraham's sacrifice of his son. Eid Al-Fitr, is the "Celebration of Fast Breaking" following Ramadan, a month-long period of fasting from sunrise to sunset. Islamic holidays are based on the lunar calendar and occur eleven days earlier each year; thus, over a period of thirty-three years, the holidays will have occurred in every month.

Although not a holiday or festival, *hajj* is an important part of Islamic life. The pilgrimage of Muslims to Mecca, *hajj* is an obligation for all Muslims to perform once in their adult lives. A person undertaking the *hajj* is required to be a confessing Muslim who has reached at least the age of puberty. Amir Ali took his wife and children to Saudi Arabia so that they could experience *hajj*.

Lisa and her family observe some of the Hindu holidays in their home. Occurring in the late fall, Diwali is a festival of lights similar to the Jewish Hanukkah. There is another festival in the spring for a good harvest. "Raksha Badahn is a ritual in Hinduism where a sister ties a string around her brother's wrists, asking him to look out for her and take care of her. It usually takes place in August," Lisa says. In India, the major Hindu festivals differ from caste to caste.

The religious beliefs of a family can influence everyday life. According to Father Michael Place, there is a great variety of life-styles in Catholic homes because of the wide range of cultural and ethnic differences. "The Catholic family is characterized by a sense of love and caring, an awareness of God, prayer, a desire to reinforce the spirit and love of Jesus, and a resolve to be a part of the Catholic faith community," Father Place says.

To Elena, the characteristics of a Catholic home are "belief in Jesus Christ and the faith that he revealed to the world through the Catholic Church. Catholics are people who observe the rules of the Catholic Church, attend mass on Sunday, and observe the holy days. A Catholic family would be anti-abortion. But primarily it would have a belief in Christ."

"Belief is one thing, observance is another," Elena continues. "Christ permeates everything I do. We have crucifixes in our home. We have Madonnas. We have Christmas. My family and I are active in the parish. Our son sings in the choir."

When asked what makes a family Catholic, Nick replies, "Catholicism would say you have to obey the rules, follow the rules, to be Catholic. I was raised that way, and I carry those beliefs with me. It doesn't change the beliefs, and it doesn't change the strength that those rules give me, but I wouldn't say that we have a Catholic home. Yet anyone walking into our home might mistake us for that because the traditions are the same."

Father Mark Elliott says that the Orthodox family practices their faith in the home. "The home is a church, too," he says. Home observance includes prayer at meals, scripture studies, observance of all feasts and fasts, and a visible presence of faith such as icons on the wall. "There should be a commitment to growth in faith as a family, not just as an individual."

In the Eastern Orthodox home, observance of feasts and fasts is stricter than in the Catholic or Protestant home. The major feast is Easter, preceded by a forty-day Lenten period and Holy Week. On the weekly fast days, Wednesday and Friday, no meat, dairy products, or even oil for the strictest, are consumed. Other fasts and feasts are marked throughout the year, including fast days before Christmas.

"In a Christian home, members of the family believe in Jesus Christ and talk about Jesus Christ," says Protestant minister Donna Gray. "There is prayer at bedtime and at one or more meals. The family worship together. The children attend church school. The family observe the principles of the Old and New Testaments of the Bible and the moral values, the Ten Commandments, and the Grand Commandment, 'Do unto your neighbor as you would have him do unto you.' There is a Bible in the home. The family shares an appreciation of the religious side of Christmas, Easter, and even Thanksgiving.

"A Catholic home differs from a Protestant home in that Catholics are more observant of the religious calendar than Protestants. They give more importance to days such as Ash Wednesday and Ascension. Catholic prayers differ, too. Catholics use the rosary and the sign of the cross. A Catholic home has more pictures or statues of Jesus and

Mary and more crucifixes. Catholics are still proud to have a child become a nun or priest. First communion is very important.

"There are differences outside the home, too. For instance, the Protestant Church holds open communion. Anyone who believes in Jesus Christ may take communion. This is not true in the Roman Catholic Church. There, one must be Catholic to receive communion."

Claudia, a Protestant married to a Catholic, has noticed some of these contrasts in her own home. "In my opinion, the only differences between a Catholic and a Protestant home are the holy days that Catholics observe," she says. "Catholics go to church on Ash Wednesday and other holy days. Protestants don't observe meatless Fridays during Lent. That's a Catholic tradition, not a Protestant tradition."

In Christianity, most religious activity is centered in the church. In Judaism, more of the observances are centered in the home with the family.

According to Rabbi Gedalia Dov Schwartz, the following factors characterize a traditional Jewish home: observance of all Jewish laws and customs, including keeping kosher, observing the sabbath and other Jewish holidays, maintaining family purity, being moral and ethical, studying the Torah and other Jewish sources, and giving charity.

Conservative Rabbi Vernon Kurtz says that characteristics of a Jewish home include Jewish ritual and artistic symbols; observance of *Shabbat*, Jewish holidays, and kashruth (keeping kosher); acknowledgment of learning by having books in the home; and a value system.

According to Rabbi Stephen Hart, three components characterize a Jewish home: objects and symbols, utilization of these items, and values. Jewish objects and symbols that are important include, among other things, a mezuzah (a small prayer scroll affixed to the doorpost of a house), seder plate for the Passover, nine-branched Hanukkah menorah, *Kiddush* cup, sabbath candleholder, and Jewish books. It is important that these objects be utilized, not just looked at. *Shabbat* should be observed. There should be a Passover seder.

Thirteen-year-old Annie put it simply, "What makes our home and family Jewish is learning about the Jewish religion and then practicing those things we have learned."

Renee believes that a Jewish family is one that observes the teachings of the Torah—faith, study, and charity— celebrates the holidays, and lives by those principles. "We sustain our religious heritage by sending our children to religious school, going to the synagogue, and observing the sabbath and Jewish holidays," Renee says. "Getting together with the family for religious holidays is important. We also do things around the synagogue, social action, such as bringing in food for the homeless. It was important to maintain my heritage. When you're raised Jewish, you are told the only way this religion has survived 5,000 years is by people keeping their faith. Otherwise it would have been gone thousands of years ago."

According to Amir Ali, Muslims pray five times a day. In a Muslim home, the family pray together whenever possible, but always at the morning prayer, which is followed by study. No smoking, alcohol, or drugs are allowed in a Muslim home. Islamic family members are not allowed to have pornographic or profane material. Children do not go to birthday parties or other social functions. Teens do not date or go to mixed parties.

"In a Buddhist home, the family is thankful for what they have been offered," Helen explains. "Karma brings us what is deserved. We don't pray for things, but we do show gratitude to Buddha for what we have." Michelle believes that a Buddhist home and family are characterized by following the Eastern traditions and philosophies. Communication with other Buddhists is also important.

Many Hindu homes have a shrine where prayers are offered every morning and evening. Worship is part of the family's daily routine. Hindu parents are obliged to teach their children right from wrong, to be sure they are educated, to help get them married at the right age, and to see that they receive their inheritance at the right time.

"In our home, Hinduism is more a way of life," Lisa explains. "It gives reasons for things. When you can explain things, it gives you hope. It is not a rigid religion that says, well, you have to go church every Sunday. It is very open-minded, the way we practice it."

Lisa's father, Lee, agrees. "It's a way of life. It's a culture. It gives you peace of mind."

Almost all religions encourage parents to see that their children receive a religious education, perhaps at the house of worship, but most important, at home.

"Religious education starts in the home," says Frank Hannigan. "The most important teachers are parents. They have to be the model that children follow by attending church, helping others, and being honest."

"Christian children should have a religious education, know Christian values, and know the Christian story," Claudia says.

Matt says, "I was raised like any other Catholic child in my neighborhood. There was Sunday attendance at church, followed by the weekly CCD (Children's Christian Development) class, and the annual celebration of Christmas, Easter, and other Christian holidays."

Lee believes that religious training helps to instill values in children. "If my children happened to see a blind person, see someone in need, I am sure they would intervene. They would not sit on the side and just observe. I think they have enough religious training to speak up against injustice."

"Our goal was that they love each other, that they be respectful. It just came from within us, not from any outside source," Roslyn adds.

Most religions do have value systems that children and teens learn in the home and in the house of worship. Frank Hannigan says Catholicism is not too different from many religions in expecting people to be virtuous and to believe in God. Catholics can be characterized by a belief in Jesus Christ and the gospels and actions based on those beliefs, as well as respect for parents and children, helping people, and giving to others. "The church community does not expect perfection," he says.

"The Jewish person should live by high ideals, incorporating Jewish ritual and behavior in everyday life, and motivated by belief in God," says Rabbi Kurtz.

The values lived through the home and family and the values taught to the children make up an important part of the Jewish home. The values should be consistent with those of Judaism. One is *Shalom Bayit* or peace in the home, focusing on how difficulties are resolved, according to Rabbi Hart.

A Reform rabbi says, "Being a good Jew means not only being a good person, but also observing all the traditions of Judaism."

"Religion gives you guidance, but it shouldn't be the

rules. Religious background keeps you in line, but it shouldn't be the be-all and end-all of life. Don't use it as an excuse to be prejudiced or bigoted," Lisa says.

One universal value is respect for parents and elders. One of the Ten Commandments is, "Honor thy mother and father." When children honor and respect parents, they have a sense of community and a sense of history and tradition.

"In Hinduism, certain values influence how you interact with your family," Roslyn says. "They include respect for elders and each other in the family unit. How you treat your older brother, how you treat your younger brother, how you treat your sister, every relationship has its special place that is more of a religious aspect to life."

Lisa says, "That's universal in India. Old people don't go to nursing homes there."

"I have very strong feelings about children respecting their elders," Lee says. "That kind of belief does carry you through, because it is backed by a message. We love our children. All we can do is wish them well and give them our blessing and love them. Their task is to respect us and our wishes. That is what is really missing in society today."

"In India, Hindu women don't work," Lee continues. "They stay home and take care of the family unit. That is an investment in your children. If that is what you call religion, the investment of a lot of love and tenderness, along with firmness and discipline, too, it's all part of the process."

In India, the Hindu family is interdependent. The parents take care of the son while he is growing up. Then the son takes care of the parents after he has reached maturity.

Buddhism holds a similar philosophy. The child is

supported by the parents until maturity; then he becomes their support. The child also pledges to observe family traditions and to be worthy of the Buddhist heritage.

"All religions have a code of ethics, whether it's called the Ten Commandments or the Seven Step program," Roslyn says. "Whatever the religions call their paths, they're really much the same. They have an ethical code giving law and order to society. All religions want you to be good and to be kind to each other. If you do that, you're religious. So if people ask me if I am religious, I say yes."

Religion in the home is an important part of life for many families, whether they are same-faith or interfaith. Karen and Nick agree that religion is something more than what you learn in a church or synagogue. "It has to be," Karen says. "If it only exists in the church or synagogue, it won't survive."

CHAPTER 4

Whose Religion
Is It, Anyway?

Glenn and his Uncle Fred stood by the door watching Glenn's children playing in the yard. Fred turned to Glenn and casually said, "Glenn, you are Jewish and Melanie is Christian. What are your children going to be?"

Glenn smiled and replied, "Human beings, I should hope."

Many of the important decisions that interfaith couples must make—and the problems those decisions cause— are child-centered. One of the most important and one of the most difficult decisions an interfaith couple must make is what will be the religious identity of their children. "If interfaith couples didn't have children, they wouldn't have any problems," a social worker who counsels interfaith couples once said, only half kidding.

Some couples decide before marriage how they will

raise their children. A person may even refuse to marry unless the partner agrees to raise the children in a certain religion. Other parents postpone making that decision or never make it at all.

"I didn't think of religious identity as an issue before I was married," Claudia says. "But once you start raising children, you start wanting your own beliefs, wanting the way you grew up to be passed on to your kids. It doesn't always work out that way, so it isn't easy."

People outside the family may have a mistaken idea of how a person's religious identity should be expressed. Some people believe that certain facial features or names are associated with a particular religious identity. "My neighbor asked me, if I am a Christian, how come I don't go to church," says eleven-year-old Zachary, who is being brought up Catholic and Jewish.

Eighteen-year-old Matt reports similar comments. "When friends of mine see me in church every Sunday, they always ask me, 'Why do you go to church so much if you're half Jewish?'"

Sandy, who grew up in an interfaith home and is now the mother of an interfaith family, says, "When I had a Jewish-sounding last name, people assumed I was Jewish. Now that my name sounds more Christian, people say that I'm not Jewish."

Susie Peterson walked into the classroom and dropped her books on the desk with a loud bang. Jenny Adler, who was reading, jumped. "Susie," she said, "what's going on? You look angry." Jenny and Susie had been friends since third grade. They had gone to Jewish religious school together and were in the youth group at the Reform Jewish synagogue. Both girls were from interfaith families.

"I'm really angry," Susie said, her hands on her hips.

"I don't know how some people can be so stupid. My math teacher just insisted that I couldn't be Jewish because my last name is Peterson." Susie retrieved a pencil that fallen to the floor. "I guess I shouldn't be surprised. My mother has been Jewish all her life, and she even teaches Jewish religious school, but someone once told her she couldn't be Jewish with a name like Peterson."

The religious makeup of an interfaith family can take many forms. The children may be brought up in the religion of the mother, the father, or both parents. No religion may be practiced in the home. If one parent converts to the religion of the other parent, that makes a difference in how the children are brought up.

Cheryl portrays her family as "very much Jewish." Cheryl knew even before she married Patrick—who is Protestant and the son of an Episcopal minister—that she wanted to raise her children Jewish. Shortly after their first son was born, Patrick converted to Judaism.

Russell describes his family concisely. "We're Jewish and Christian because my Dad's Christian." Russell and his two sisters are being raised Jewish.

Gary, who was brought up as a Presbyterian, and Michelle, raised as a Buddhist, are bringing up their children Buddhist. Michelle says, "Our older child, Brad, identifies himself as a Buddhist. Our younger child, Amy, embarrassedly acknowledges her Buddhist beliefs. She is probably more embarrassed by her ethnicity than her religion. Brad is proud of both his Christian and Buddhist background."

Children become aware of religious identity at an early age. At age three, when Zachary first realized that his parents were of different religions, the questions started. "But we have been open about it only in the past three years," says Zachary's mother, Karen. "We began really talking with him more since he started school. Questions were generated at school by students and by the school itself. When Zachary came home, 'What am I?' was the first question."

Children do not have to be confused about their religious identity, even when each parent has a different religion. Renee says, "It was very clear from the beginning that the children and I are Jewish and Daddy is Christian. We respect Daddy for what he is. But we have chosen to be a Jewish family. Roger participates one hundred percent."

Roger agrees. "The children are very clear about their religious identity. There is no confusion."

Eric is Catholic; his wife, Claudia, is Protestant. Their sons have been baptized in the Catholic Church, but they have attended both churches. "Our children know there are differences in our religions," Claudia says. "They know there's Mom's church and Dad's church; even Dad's and Peter's church, and David's, James's and Mom's church. I don't know if they know the difference between Catholic and Protestant."

When twelve-year-old Kevin was younger, he wondered why he and his brother were not of both religions, since they had one Christian and one Jewish parent. "Most people considered us to be both," he says. "However, Mom and Dad told us that they decided to raise us Jewish." When people ask Kevin what is his religion, Kevin answers, "Jewish." But Kevin's younger brother, Barry, says, "Both."

"Well," Kevin admits, "sometimes I say I'm a little bit Christian, but mostly Jewish."

Eighteen-year-old Stacey identifies herself as Jewish; her sixteen-year-old brother, Brent, says he is both Jewish and Christian. "I'm half and half," Brent says. "It sort of depends on the day, whether I feel Jewish. We have a tree at Christmas, but I also have a Jewish education."

"It's ironic," Stacey says. "My roommate is from an interfaith family. Even though her mother converted to Judaism because her father was much more conservative, she still considers herself of both religions. She is not both, but she gets attention by saying she is. I am literally from a family that is both, and I say I'm Jewish."

Matt doesn't hedge. "Religion is based on upbringing, personal decisions, and personal beliefs," he says. "Although my mother is Catholic and my father is Jewish, I am not half-Catholic and half-Jewish. I am one hundred percent Roman Catholic, based on my upbringing and personal beliefs."

Most experts agree that interfaith parents should choose a religious identity for their children, and that the choice should be made early, when the child is young or even before the child is born. "If a couple plan to have children, they should decide even before marriage what religion they will follow, what holidays they will observe, and how they will relate to their families," says social worker Tema Rosenblum.

"Many couples postpone thinking ahead about religious issues until the child is born," says Donna Gray, a Protestant minister. "If one partner is Catholic, they want the child baptized right away, so the issue of religion comes up. More couples are opting to do nothing because they can't decide."

It is not easy to decide what religion a child should follow. Both parents have a personal stake in the religion in which they grew up. However, many interfaith parents do make that decision and do choose to follow just one religion. It takes time, and it's not easy. "We both wanted our children to be of a single religion," Lynn says. "We agreed that being of two religions is being of no religion." Lynn and Richard decided, in theory, on their children's religious identity before they were married. "But in reality we made that decision some time after Kevin was born. It's a lot easier to make a decision in theory. We both grew up in what we considered to be religious environments, and we both wanted our children to have a religion."

"Before we had children, Richard agreed to raise them Jewish," Lynn continues. "But once Kevin was born and Richard was really a father, he felt very differently about it. He tried to find something that would make us both happy, some kind of compromise religion that would make us comfortable with all the traditions put together. It simply doesn't exist to our knowledge, so we needed to make a decision. Richard was more willing to compromise than I was."

"I had lost interest in going back and becoming active in the church," Richard says. "I didn't really want to do all the things that would be necessary to raise the boys as Christians, such as taking them to Sunday school. I already had more than enough education."

"Deciding that the boys were going to be Jewish was the most difficult decision," Lynn says. "We studied other religions as much as we could. But emotionally I just wasn't prepared to let go. The basic decision was not easy; but, once we decided, the rest just seemed to fall into place."

"When I became a mother was when I decided I wanted to raise my children Jewish," Renee says. "It was as if something turned on inside of me when I gave birth. All this identity came gushing out."

"It was a tough decision; it was very tough," Marilyn says. "I didn't feel capable of raising the children anything but Jewish. I was perfectly willing to let Larry raise them as Protestants, but he did not have any interest in that. I was not willing to raise them Protestant and go to church with them, because that went against everything I'd been brought up with. I was willing to raise them Jewish, so I guess by a process of elimination, we made our decision. It wasn't based on deep philosophical things, it was based on practical considerations."

"The fact that my whole family lives here made it easier to raise the children as Jews," says Debbie, who is married to a Protestant. "If we lived where Mitch's family is, we might have gone along with his religion, because his parents are strong in their religion. But since my whole family live here, it was easier to identify with them."

Some interfaith parents do not make a definite decision on religious identity, or they decide to follow no particular religion. Michelle, who was brought up Buddhist, says that she and her husband, Gary, who was raised as a Christian, never even thought about the religion of their children. "I'm not sure there was ever a *conscious* decision about what religion our children should have," Michelle says. "We felt that moral behavior and development were more important than following a specific religion, and we discussed that at length."

"Because I am Jewish and my husband, Lee, is Hindu, we told our children that they are Hinjews," Roslyn says with a smile.

Lee also comes from an interfaith home. His father was Hindu and his mother was Sikh, another Eastern religion. "I go to both temples, two completely different temples," Lee says. "We tried to bring up our children with respect for all religions."

"That's right," Lee's daughter, Lisa, says. "We go to synagogue with our friends, and we go to the Hindu temple to see our friends. My brothers and I believe different things. The older brother is the most Hindu, even though he is dating a Catholic girl. The younger brother is the most philosophical. I am in between. If this sounds good or that sounds good, that's what I believe; whatever works."

Sandy says, "I made a very conscious decision to raise my children to be human beings in the world. That allows that there are different ways to the truth. It's been both a success and a failure. It's harder that way."

The grandparents may put pressure on the parents to make a decision about the religious identity of the children. Nick says, "Before Karen and I were married, my parents asked me how we were going to raise the children. I said we hadn't made a decision. They asked me again when Zachary was born. I said we hadn't make a decision. When Zachary was seven, my mother asked what our plans were. They don't ask anymore."

Sometimes it is difficult for the grandparents to accept the religious identity choice that is made for their grandchildren. "My mother would have been happier if the boys were baptized and were going to church," Richard says.

Richard's wife, Lynn, says, "I think to some extent Richard's mother now accepts things the way they are.

But when our second son was born, she said, 'Well, maybe one can be Lutheran and one can be Jewish.' Comments like that came up from time to time. Now she really accepts it, because this is the way it is. Of course, *my* parents are thrilled that the children are being brought up Jewish."

Greek Orthodox priest Father Mark Elliott explains that there may be pressure from the grandparents to baptize a child in the Orthodox faith. A lot is at stake. "If you do have him baptized, the child will be raised in the Orthodox faith; if not, the child will not receive the sacraments," Father Mark says.

Patrick's father, an Episcopal minister, wished that Patrick's children would be brought up Christian. "However, he did agree that it was better for the children to have only one religion in the household," Patrick says.

Some parents do follow the advice of the grandparents in making religious identity decisions. Others consult with religious leaders or social workers. Many depend on the advice of friends, especially those who have interfaith families of their own. One mother says, "It was important for us to find out from other interfaith couples how they made their decisions. The answers were along the lines of what feels comfortable, who is stronger in the family, whose sense of religiousness is stronger."

Many religious leaders and social workers, as well as parents, believe that a child cannot be brought up with two religions. They agree that children should be raised in the tradition of one parent, with respect for the other parent's tradition. A rabbi expressed this feeling: "I believe in the parents declaring one way or the other or not to choose at all. But I don't believe that you can do it both ways."

"It is extremely difficult to raise a child in both faiths," says the Reverend Donna Gray. "It is too confusing to the child. Start the children in one faith. They may go to another when they are older. Express to your children why you believe in Jesus Christ; or, if you don't, why you don't. Let your children know how you feel."

Father Mark Elliott recalls a young man who wanted his child to be baptized in the Catholic Church but confirmed in the Greek Orthodox Church. Father Mark could not agree to that. "It is not good," he says. "A family should take one course and not confuse the child. It is better to be raised as a good Catholic than a bad Orthodox."

Rabbi Herbert Bronstein also advises against raising a child in two faiths. "If the parents can't decide, they shouldn't throw it at the children. It's not just for religious reasons, but for psychological reasons as well." Rabbi Bronstein has counseled young adults who are still upset and confused over their dual religious background.

"Raise them in one. Don't raise them in two; don't raise them in none," is the advice of a minister. "But don't forget that the other faith is part of a child's history, too."

Religious identity may be more confusing to those children who are brought up in the religions of both parents, or who must decide their religious beliefs for themselves. But some parents believe that this is the best course and are attempting to follow it.

Karen and Nick are raising their son, Zachary, as both Catholic and Jewish. Whenever Zachary asked questions about the difference between Catholicism and Judaism, Nick answered diplomatically. "I didn't want to color his feelings toward either religion by saying, I think that this is the right one, Mother thinks that is the right one. I was trying not to confuse him as he entered what would be a confusing period. At the same time, neither one of us wanted to say that the other parent's religion is not right."

"When Zachary asked, 'What am I?' we told him that he was Jewish and Catholic," Karen says. "It felt like coming out of the closet. Until then there hadn't been much discussion about it. We kept the conversations separate. There were Jewish-oriented conversations and Catholic conversations, but we had never brought the two together. It's not that trying to do both is wrong; we were just afraid of confronting the issue. We kind of danced around it, trying to do both, and trying to be kind to each other's religion.

"For Zachary to have gone one way or another would have declared him as one religion or another. And we were trying so hard to help him to be both. We've just done our best to share."

Nick agrees. "He will never be raised in one religion."

In the Catholic-Protestant family, children may be brought up in both Christian traditions by trying to find the commonality of both. That requires religious education and attendance at religious celebrations in both churches, ecumenical baptisms with clergy from both churches officiating, and intercommunion, receiving communion in the Protestant church (Catholicism forbids non-Catholics to receive communion in a Catholic church).

Claudia, a Protestant married to a Catholic, thinks it is important that their children be raised as Christians. "It is less important whether it is Protestant or Catholic," she says.

Claudia's husband, Eric, agrees. "Our focus is to make sure our children are brought up Christian, to have the same kind of quality and concerns that a good person does, and not get wound up in the differences between Catholic and Protestant. I think many of the differences are more social than religious."

Some parents believe they should expose their children to both religions and allow the children to decide which to follow. However, most parents, as well as child development and religious professionals, believe that it is not wise to let the children choose their religion.

Those who believe children should choose say that these are merely different religions—not one right and one wrong; therefore, the child should choose. "Let the child try both religions," they say. "Children should be exposed to both religions."

Others advise that one of the responsibilities of parenthood is choosing for the children. A child wants limits and wants the parents to make decisions. Parents should make these decisions before children are born, even before marriage, if possible. "It's expecting too much of a seven-year-old," Janie says. "If Tom and I had problems making this decision, how can you expect children to choose? You can't ask them to choose, because they are choosing between Mommy and Daddy."

"Don't put the child in the middle," says Felice Friedman, a social worker who counsels interfaith families. "It should be made clear that the children are not choosing Mom or Dad by their religious identity." A parent can be disappointed and hurt when his or her religion is not the one chosen by the child.

Mitch and his family agree with that viewpoint. Discussing religious identity with his wife, Debbie, and teenage children, Stacey and Brent, Mitch says, "You've learned only one religion, in a sense. I didn't go to church every Sunday, and I didn't take you with me. You have never been forced to make a choice. We made the choice for you. We never asked you to choose at any point in time. You didn't have to say, 'Gee, I think I'll go with Dad this week, and Mom next week.'"

"If we had to choose between our parents, that would be bad," sixteen-year-old Brent agrees.

"When someone is born into a single-faith family, they're told to believe something. It's coming from both parents, and that is what they ultimately have to believe," eighteen-year-old Stacey says. "I was given insight into both."

Brent responds, "How many people are actually going to choose their religion? Most people just get born, and their parents teach them what they are. No one really gets to choose."

"You get to hear both sides, but you're not exactly choosing, either," says Debbie, Brent's mother.

"But you left it up to us to choose later on," Stacey says.

"That's right," Mitch responds. "You received the religious education. Now it's your choice to reject it or accept it."

Annie was given the option to decide whether she wanted to go to religious school, but she was not given the choice of religion. Glenn, her father, would not have been comfortable with anything other than Judaism. "From the beginning of our marriage, we agreed to raise our children Jewish," Glenn says. "When the children are older, they can decide for themselves."

Although most experts advise against letting children choose their religious identity, they also say a child should learn about other religions. Protestant minister David Tracy says, "Once the decision is made about which religion the child will be, the family can relax. Then the child can explore other religions without the parents feeling threatened."

A child should have exposure to other religions, not as an option for identity, but as a learning experience. Interfaith children already observe the different religions of their relatives and friends, so they should have the opportunity to understand other religions and appreciate them. Children need to learn about the religions of both parents because that is part of their makeup. Each parent is entitled to his or her own religious identity, even if it is not the same as the children's. "I'm raising my child Jewish, but I am still a Christian," one woman said. "Why should I give up my Christian life just because my husband and children are Jewish?"

Michelle agrees with the idea of exposing children to religions other than their own. "Since we attend the Buddhist temple, the children know more about Buddhism," she says. "But we also tell them Christian stories, as well as family stories about their father's Protestant childhood."

"They can understand that this is what others do. It can be an enriching experience, part of an education," says one father. "Religion is not contagious. If identity is strong, the child won't be swayed."

"Exposure to the other parent's religion is very healthy," another says. "It opens their eyes. It is healthy, positive, and good. If a child has strong sense of identity, he cannot be harmed."

Eighteen-year-old Matt believes it is his obligation to learn about the Jewish faith, the religion of his father. "Although I am a devout Catholic, I think it would not be right to ignore the faith of an entire half of my family and my background."

"There are limits," a Jewish father says. "I would never take my child to Catholic mass. But we do participate in my wife's family traditions such as Easter dinner and decorating the Christmas tree."

The way the parents feel about their religions as adults influences their choice of religious identity for their children. The way they were brought up themselves also influences their choice. Cheryl was brought up in an interfaith family as a secular or nonreligious Jew. She never quite felt she belonged to either the Jewish or Christian community. That was why, even before she was married or had children, Cheryl decided that she would raise her children as Jews in a Jewish home.

Richard was also influenced by his own religious background. "I was not unhappy with the religion I was exposed to," Richard says. "But I was much less interested in it. It is more important for Lynn to be involved in things that are Jewish, to maintain that connection, and to have Jewish children. So it made more sense to raise the children Jewish."

When Glenn was growing up, being Jewish was more a form of identity than a religion. His father was not religious. His mother was secular and disdained religion. "I grew up learning that it is important to show you're a Jew," Glenn says. "The world will keep reminding you, anyway."

Nick goes along with the ethnicity idea. "You're born Jewish, you may get a religious education, and you may go to temple; but even if you don't, you are just as Jewish as those who do," he says. "Not so in Catholicism. You are born nothing, you are made Catholic, and you only remain Catholic if you play by the rules. To a Catholic, not to be Catholic is a big problem. But you can't *not* be Jewish, you are born into it. Even if you're not a practicing Jew, you are still Jewish."

The problems with religious identity depend on the strength of religious identity of the two parents, according to Felice Friedman. If one partner has a strong religious persuasion and the other does not, the child will probably be brought up in the religion of the parent with the stronger identity.

The faith chosen should be the one that is most active. "If the Catholic partner is not active in religion, but the Lutheran partner is, the child should be brought up Lutheran," says Frank Hannigan.

Tema Rosenblum says, "The parents need to choose and to explain to the child why they made this decision. They must say, 'We have decided and agreed,' and show a united front."

"Identity is not just religion, it is attitudes and feelings," Marilyn says. "It's much more than observances. It's a whole mind-set, looking at things in a Jewish way. When my children hear about the Holocaust, they look at it in a different way than a Christian child does because they have a sense of identification. When they go downtown at Christmas and see Santa Claus, they say, 'That's for Christian kids, we don't believe that.' It's a whole orientation."

In some interfaith families, the parents do not have the choice of religious identity for their children. Because of a strong religious policy, the decision is made for them. For instance, in an Islamic family, even if the mother is not Muslim, the children must be raised as Muslims. The Catholic Church encourages mixed-marriage couples of which one partner is Catholic to bring up their children as Catholics.

In Orthodox and Conservative Judaism, only interfaith children whose mothers are Jewish are identified as

Jewish. In Reform Judaism, a child is considered Jewish if either parent is Jewish, and the child is brought up as a Jew in a Jewish home and with a Jewish education.

"However the family decide to raise the children, it should be private. It should be within the family," says Lisa, who recently married a man of another faith. "How Jeb and I raise our children should be our decision and our choice. Our children should not be subjected to questions from others."

Most clergy and social workers agree that, no matter how or when a religion is chosen, a child needs that identity. Frank Hannigan summed it up: "A child must have some faith, some faith to act on."

"The Catholic priest said that we ought to make a decision," Karen says. "He suggested that we first get a sense of our own feelings of religiousness. We started to go to church every other Sunday, and we tried a couple of synagogues. We are not practicing religiously, but we recognize that there is a need to have something at home."

"We thought that it was important for the children to have an identity religiously," Marilyn says. "Everyone says, 'I'm this, I'm that.' I wanted them to have an identity for the time being so that when they got older they could do what they wanted with it. At least they had something, they had some religious education and some identity. That was a satisfying solution for us."

"Parents need to talk about religion with their children, even if they are not religious or do not believe in religion," says the Reverend Donna Gray. "Children have a natural spirituality. If they do not learn about religion from their parents, they will pick something up from the media and will be left to their own resources and create their own ideas."

Social worker Mimi Dunitz says, "You have to make a choice for your child, whether Judaism or some other religion, so the child has a strong religious identity. The other parent does not have to lose his or her identity. The child should know about the other religion and understand it. A child needs to *be* something."

Building
Relationships

"**Z**achary is almost twelve now, and I think my father is finally beginning to accept our interfaith family and the way we are raising Zachary," Karen says. "But there have been moments when I got a little nervous.

"When Zachary was in kindergarten, he came home one day and told me, 'I learned to say grace.' I had a fleeting moment of fear. That's what I felt, fear. He said the word 'grace,' so I thought it was something about Jesus. Even though we are bringing him up both Catholic and Jewish, I still felt fear. But Zachary said, 'God is great, God is good, we thank Him for this food.' It was so simple, I don't know why I got scared.

"A few months later, we went to my parents' home for dinner. It was Thanksgiving, and we wanted to say a blessing before the meal. Somebody mentioned that Zachary knew how to say grace. I looked at my father, and I could tell that he was going through the same moment of doubt. He looked very angry, as if wondering, 'What is he going to come out with?' And then he was relieved, just as I was, when Zachary said, 'God is great, God is good, we thank Him for this food.'"

Whatever the religious makeup of an interfaith family, even if one parent has converted to the religion of the other parent, there will be relatives and friends who do not share the same beliefs. Interfaith children have to interact with grandparents, cousins, and friends. That means relating to people with not only a variety of religious beliefs and ethnic backgrounds, but also different attitudes toward the interfaith family.

Next to the parents, the grandparents probably have the most influence on the children in an interfaith family. How the grandparents interact with them depends on a variety of factors. The grandparents' attitudes toward intermarriage, their own religious choices and family background, their previous relationships with their children, and even where they live affect the way grandparents relate to interfaith grandchildren.

The relationship is influenced as much by the personalities of the grandparents as by the religious choice of the interfaith family. Renee's parents are older than Roger's parents and do not participate in many family activities. "Roger's mother and stepfather are the real grandparents," Renee says. "They relate very well; they're very supportive."

"My family have tried very hard," Roger says. "Even though they are Christian, when they are in town they go to the synagogue with our family. I could not have asked for more support."

"I've never been very close to my father," Patrick says.

Although his father lives nearby, Patrick sees him only at Christmas and Easter and a few other times during the year. "My father is not a particularly warm person, but I enjoy it when we get together. I realize that, because he is an Episcopal minister, it's hard for him to have his grandchildren brought up in a different religion. His parishioners want to meet the children because he always talks about them, leaving out the fact that they are Jewish. Religion is such an important part of my father's life that he is disappointed not to be able to bring his grandchildren into that environment."

Cheryl's father is not close to his grandchildren, but her mother is very close. Cheryl's grandfather lives with her mother. "We see them at least once a week. Mother is the closest of all," Cheryl says.

"My in-laws are very religious and very serious people," Debbie says. "They don't make jokes and laugh; they don't drink or dance. They live a totally different life than we do. That's why I said, you can't put me in that situation. I couldn't have lived in that situation and been a good wife. I couldn't have been a happy person."

Often the parents of interfaith couples struggle with the marriage of their children, and especially with how their grandchildren will be raised. Eventually, most accept the marriage, the family, and the grandchildren. Karen's Jewish parents have been concerned about their grandson Zachary and his upbringing. "We have been putting them off for so long, they don't even ask anymore about things like bar mitzvah," Karen says.

Greta was not pleased when her son married a Catholic woman who did not convert. "Although my son and daughter-in-law said they would bring up the children Jewish, I was still concerned it couldn't be done," Greta says. "I am more used to it now, but it has taken time."

Father Mark Elliott says that when someone marries an Orthodox person, they are "marrying the whole family." There may be a lot of pressure from the Orthodox grandparents to do things their way.

Other grandparents accept the situation more readily. Gary, who was raised as a Protestant but is now following the Buddhist religion of his wife, found this to be true. "My mother and father gladly received this new way of life because it isn't really new to them. We lived in Japan in the '60s," Gary says. "There was never any pressure from either my parents or Michelle's parents to do anything in a particular way religiously. If anyone perceived problems with our family, it was my own grandparents."

Roslyn says, "My parents had no problem with my relationship with Lee. In fact, my father gave my phone number to Lee when we met, which was at a Jewish wedding. On the other hand, relatives in the extended family had a problem with it. I lost connections with a lot of my relatives. The relatives were Orthodox Jews, my own parents were not."

"Actually, my family is quite democratic," says Lee, whose father is Hindu and mother is Sikh. "My mother believes in something; my dad believes in something. My sister and my brother, they all believe in their own things. They have temples for worship in their own houses. My mother had a cross in her house at one time. I think that these people are more like my gurus, my teachers."

Fifteen-year-old Josh must deal with a variety of relationships from three sides: his father's Jewish family, his mother's interfaith family where she was raised as a Catholic, and his stepfather's Protestant family. Josh says he has no problems with his father's family. "But I know that there were conflicts between them and my mother, and conflicts still exist."

Josh's mother, Sandy, agrees. "They are not quite sure about these kids. They're very good to them, but these kids are not quite full-fledged members of that family because I'm their mother. My own parents think they are great; that's not an issue with them. With their stepfather's family, I don't think religion is an issue so much as their being stepchildren."

Of course, some never accept the interfaith marriage and families of their children. Benjamin, who was brought up Jewish, married a Catholic woman. They have three children that they are raising Catholic. It is very hard for Benjamin's father, Arnold, to accept this situation, and he won't talk to Benjamin. On the other hand, Arnold has accepted the intermarriage of his daughter, Beth, because Beth is raising her children in the Jewish faith.

Roger felt a lot of friction from Renee's parents. "They were trying to make me fit the Jewish mold," he says. "There is still never a call from her parents on Christmas. I have never been recognized as Christian."

Some interfaith parents are afraid the grandparents may be too influential in the child's religious upbringing. "I would never leave my children with their Catholic grandparents," a Jewish man said. "I'm afraid they would take the children right across the street to the church and have them baptized."

Geographical location is also an important factor in the relationship between grandparents and grandchildren. There is little contact between Elizabeth's Islamic family and her Christian parents because her parents live a long distance away.

In other situations, grandparents may live in the same state, the same city, or even the same house as the interfaith family. It's that way for Helen, who was brought up as a Christian and married Robert, who is a Buddhist. They are bringing up their children as Buddhists. Helen's mother, who lives with them, still practices Christianity, going to church and celebrating the Christian holidays.

"Lee's mother, who was Sikh, lived with us," Roslyn says. "Our children spent a lot of time with her. They would learn prayers from her. They would sit and sing with her. They may not have known what she was doing, but they got the religious feeling from her. Now they know the songs and the prayers, even in Sanskrit."

How the grandparents get along with each other is important, too. The Jewish grandmother of interfaith grandchildren says, "I have learned to accept that the other grandparents, who are Catholic, have as much right to their grandchildren as we do. The children are being brought up in a Jewish household, so I feel better about that."

"All the grandparents get along great with the children, and they get along with each other, too," Marilyn says. "And all the cousins get along well. Most of Philip and Steven's cousins are Jewish, but the cousins they see most are also from an interfaith family. The father is Greek, and the mother is Jewish, but the children are being raised Jewish. My children don't even know that their uncle is not Jewish. That family is more observant than we are. They observe Passover, their son is going to be bar mitzvahed, and they go to Hebrew school. In fact, their mother only agreed to marry on condition that they would raise the children Jewish."

"The Jewish religion has a lot of family in it," Josh says. "You go to services and then you get together with the family. We get together with my aunt and uncle. Our family does a lot of eating, eating and talking."

Children growing up in an interfaith family not only have cousins but also friends of different religions: friends from single-faith families as well as interfaith friends. Thirteen-year-old Annie has many friends from interfaith families. "My non-interfaith friends think I'm lucky because I celebrate both Christmas and Hanukkah," Annie says.

"I have a lot of friends from interfaith families," Steven says. "Most of them just call themselves Christian. We talk about religion once in a while."

Eleven-year-old Jon, who comes from a Protestant-Jewish family, says, "Most of my friends are Christian. My friends don't ask questions about my religion, but my teacher does. There's only one Jewish kid in my class, and that's me."

Lisa's Hindu-Jewish family lived in an area where there were families with a variety of religious and ethnic backgrounds. Lisa had a lot of Jewish friends. She even wanted to go Hebrew school because so many of her friends were going.

Teenagers Stacey and Brent have many friends from single-faith families, but not many from interfaith families. "Most of the people around here happen to be Jewish," Brent says. "We don't sit down and discuss religion. Actually, I don't think guys worry about religion so much, anyway. Religion plays a minor part in our lives."

Generally, young children don't discuss religion with their friends. But, as children get older and enter high school or college, religion may become a topic of conversation or discussion more often. "The issue of religion and intermarriage was avoided in public school," says twenty-three-year old Howard. "I attended a very big junior high school and high school. Lots of the kids came from homes with interfaith marriages and interfaith divorces. It was not as if everyone had two parents of the same faith and we were the odd ones out. It came up as a point of interest, nothing more. 'So one of your parents is Catholic, and one is Jewish.' It was something interesting, not something strange, that you came from an interfaith family."

Howard has friends from interfaith families as well as same-faith families. "Among my interfaith friends, the subject of religion never comes up," Howard says. "There are more questions from the non-interfaith kids. They say, 'You have a Catholic mother and a Jewish father. How were you raised?' I always laugh it off by saying, yes, we get both Hanukkah presents and Christmas presents. It's a double whammy. It's more interest than anything else. It's more like: How does that work? How do you feel about it? Our being from an interfaith family was never an issue in Sunday school or youth group either. The programs were 'you-directed.' They did not focus on your family."

"In college, I'm rooming with three people," Stacey says. "The subject of religion comes up, and I say I'm Jewish. You get into these discussions. One of my room-mates knew nothing about Judaism, and I knew nothing about Catholicism. I was writing a paper when I was on the Christian half of the religion course I was taking. I didn't understand the subject very well, and my room-mate helped me with it. We got really deep into conversation, so things like that would come up then. The more you get into conversation on religion, the more things come out."

Josh says, "I have some friends whose families don't

have any particular religion. Or the parents do, but the children don't feel they belong to it, because they have one parent who is of one religion and the other is something else."

Sandy thinks that, in her area, school cliques grow along religious lines. Matt does not agree. "We don't view our Catholic friends and our Jewish friends as different kinds of friends," Matt says. "Friends are friends, whatever background they come from. In religion they are different, but I don't think they are much different in personality. You choose friends by the kind of person they are, rather than by their religion."

Once in a while, a child or teen is teased or harassed for coming from an interfaith family. Elena vividly remembers one day when six-year-old Howard came home from kindergarten. He ran into the house and slammed the door. Tears were streaming down his face, and his hands were clenched in tight fists. "What in the world is the matter?" Elena asked as she bent down to comfort him.

Howard could hardly talk through his anger. "I hate Henry," he wailed. "Henry called me a Jatholic."

"A Jatholic?" Elena asked.

"Because my dad is Jewish, and my mom is Catholic."

Elena smiles when she recalls the scene. "Later, Howard and Henry became very good friends," she says.

Lisa discovered that sometimes it is not friends who are intolerant, but the friends' parents. She says, "Interfaith children—or any children, for that matter—should not be subjected to questions by their friends' parents, as I was. 'Oh, what are you?' My friends didn't care; they couldn't care less. It's from their parents that they learn bigotry.

They're taught, 'She's Jewish, you don't want to talk to her.' 'She's Indian, you know how they are.' And so on.

"When I first moved here, a girl down the block who was Catholic said her parents would not allow me on her property because my mom was Jewish. I didn't even know what the word property meant. I became very aware of racial injustice when we moved here."

Zachary tells about another incident. "There's this one kid in my school who's really mean; he makes fun of people," Zachary says. "He's Christian, but he doesn't make fun of me because I'm both Catholic and Jewish. He makes fun of my being Jewish. I told Mom, and Mom told the principal. The principal and I had a talk, and then the three of us had a talk. He seems to have stopped. He didn't do it very often; but when he did, he came on strong."

Matt reports that when his family was living in England, they went to the school to see a Christmas pageant. "At one point in the play, the children playing the parts of the Jews came out huddled over, grumbling, holding large amounts of bills to their chests, and grabbing at each others' money. My parents immediately said, 'Let's go,' and walked out. This was discrimination. It was my first experience of the kind, and it disturbed me that this was how some people envisioned my father, and possibly me. It was this kind of discrimination that increased my awareness of my ties to the Jewish faith. I now feel that I have a responsibility to my father and to my heritage to be aware of anti-Semitism."

A community as a whole may have a prevailing attitude toward certain religious groups as well as interfaith families. This can influence the interfaith family's choice of community. Where Roger and Renee live, many of their children's friends come from interfaith families. "It's so common in our town and our synagogue," Roger says. "This town was very attractive to us for that reason. Other places were not comfortable; they were more segregated. But here it doesn't matter. You don't even know who is and who isn't interfaith, which makes it easier for our marriage."

Lynn and Richard have settled in a similar town. "This community has so many mixed couples, there's not as much of a sense of separate Jewish and Christian social networks," Richard says. "Twenty-five percent of the families are mixed. That was one of our reasons for moving here. We didn't realize how mixed the families were, but we definitely were looking for a community that was mixed religiously, where we would both feel comfortable. Other areas were too much one way or the other. Twenty-five percent of couples in our synagogue are interfaith, and a lot of our friends are, too."

"Our city is great in that respect," says Melanie. "There is more diversity in families and schools. We purposely moved here for that reason."

Jeanette reports that her Jewish-Japanese grandchildren live in an area with a "favorable environment, where interfaith, intercultural families are accepted."

"We live in a community where half of the people send their children to Catholic school, and half don't," Elena says. "I think that because our kids go to public schools, it puts us in another community than if we had sent them to Catholic school."

"One given is that it is physically and emotionally almost impossible to live in both the Jewish and the Catholic community at the same time," Ray says. "People at our church have their social life with Catholic people. And most of the people at the synagogue—by choice, not by necessity—have their social life with other Jews.

Ray's son, Howard, agrees. "It is impossible. You can't be a member of a synagogue and be involved in the sisterhood and the men's club and the education there, and at the same time be involved in the Catholic church."

"I think that a clear disadvantage to being involved in the Catholic community has been a lack of Jewish friends," says Elena.

"We meet Jewish friends at work, or prior relationships, or school, not from the Jewish community," Ray says. "If we belonged to the synagogue and were active there, we would have Jewish friends."

"Then there would be a lack of Catholic friends," Howard remarks.

"But that was a choice; not a good choice or a bad choice, just a choice," Ray says. "Still, children of this generation are more assimilated than they were in my generation."

Whether it is belonging to a community or getting along with family and friends, everyone in an interfaith family has to deal with a variety of attitudes and degrees of acceptance. Over time, attitudes may change and acceptance may increase.

"Our parents seem to be more accepting now," Karen says.

Nick agrees. "Accepting, that's the word. All our parents have accepted what we're doing."

"Some on different levels than others," Karen adds.

"Absolutely, but each in their own way."

CHAPTER 6

The December
Dilemma and
Other Holidays

"**M**erry Christmas!" Craig shouted cheerfully the moment his grandmother opened the door. Craig and his parents, Diane and Ron, walked into the house, each carrying a stack of brightly wrapped presents. Along with the red, green, and gold packages were blue and silver ones.

As Craig and his mother placed the Christmas gifts under the tree, Ron pulled from a shopping bag a large silver Hanukkah menorah, a candleholder for nine small candles. Ron had given Diane the menorah as a present the first Christmas after they were married.

Craig's mother was Jewish. His dad was Catholic. Craig was being brought up in both religions. Ever since Craig could remember—and his mother told him it had been going on even before he was born—his parents traveled from Detroit to Milwaukee to visit his grandparents, his father's parents, for the Christmas holiday. They always brought not only Christmas gifts but Hanukkah gifts as well. And if Hanukkah occurred at the same time as Christmas, they also brought the menorah.

Craig stood back and admired the Christmas tree. It was beautiful with the colored lights. Grandma and Grandpa had some very old ornaments, things that had been made by Craig's dad and his dad's brother and sister many years before. There were also many new ornaments. It seemed as if Grandma added something new each year.

Grandma came to the dining room door. "Dinner is ready," she said, "but I know you want to light the Hanukkah candles first."

Craig's parents and grandparents gathered around the dining room table while Craig placed the candles in the menorah. He lit the middle candle first. Then, using that candle, he lit six more, because this was the sixth night of Hanukkah. Everyone sang the two blessings in Hebrew. Craig had taught his Catholic grandparents the words many years ago after he had learned them.

Craig knew that for Jews, Hanukkah was a minor holiday. But Christmas was a major and very important holiday for Christians. He enjoyed celebrating both holidays, because it emphasized the two traditions in which he was growing up. At home in Detroit, they always had a Christmas tree as well as Hanukkah decorations.

Craig watched the candles flickering brightly in the darkened dining room. At that moment, they were as pretty as the lights on the Christmas tree. Craig looked at his mother. She was staring at the candles, too. She had a slight smile on her face, but her eyes looked sad. Craig knew why. Many years ago, his mother's father—his other grandfather—had stopped coming to visit their family in December because they celebrated both the Christian and the Jewish holidays. For Craig's Jewish grandfather, this was too hard to take, so he just stayed away. Craig knew that made his mother sad, because she wanted to share the holidays with her own parents as well as her husband's parents.

A year ago, when Craig was twelve, he was first allowed to attend midnight mass with his parents and grand-parents. This year, after mass, the five sat at the kitchen table drinking hot chocolate. Diane told the family that, although she had a Jewish background, she never felt uncomfortable celebrating Christmas. "I like being a part of Ron's family," Diane said, as she patted her mother-in-law's hand. "I like all the traditions and the excitement. For me it's family, it's warmth. It's wonderful."

Religious holidays can be times of happiness, family togetherness, and sharing. In the interfaith household, holidays may also create increased tension and new problems.

Some interfaith families celebrate all the religious holidays of both faiths of the parents. "We do a lot from both religions," says Debbie, a Jewish woman married to a Christian. "We celebrate all the holidays: Easter, Christmas, Hanukkah, Passover, and of course Rosh Hashanah and Yom Kippur."

Glenn, a Jew, and his wife Melanie, who was brought up as a Baptist, are raising their children, Annie and Scott, in the Jewish tradition. They celebrate all the religious holidays except Easter. "Every holiday is an excuse to give presents, to get the family together," says

Glenn. He accepts the secular symbols of the various religious holidays.

Although Elena and Ray are raising their three sons as Catholics, the family have always informally celebrated the major Jewish holidays, recognizing Ray's Jewish heritage. As their son, eighteen-year-old Matt, explains, "Each April, we would travel to my aunt's house to celebrate Passover. In December, we lighted the Hanukkah candles with a short prayer. At the High Holidays my parents, and sometimes my brothers and I, attended services at the synagogue."

Gary, who comes from a Christian home, and Michelle, who is Buddhist, are raising their children as Buddhists. They celebrate the Buddhist holidays as well as the holidays of their Christian relatives. "The list of Buddhist celebrations is long and involved, but we do invite many people to our temple to share in some of the major holidays," Michelle says. "We also celebrate Christian and Jewish holidays in our home and enjoy the traditions. We discuss the religious significance of the Christian holidays, even Halloween and Valentine's Day, which have religious roots. We have a close family friend who is a Catholic priest. He tells us many stories."

Robert is Buddhist; his wife, Helen, grew up Christian and is now Buddhist. Helen's mother lives with them. "We celebrate the Christian holidays for my mother," Helen says. "We celebrate Christmas and Easter, and we have a Christmas tree. We celebrate the Buddhist holidays for ourselves."

In Roslyn and Lee's Jewish-Hindu home, they observe the holidays of many cultures. "We celebrate the spirit and the time of year more than the religious aspect of the holidays," their daughter Lisa says. "We celebrate Christmas, but not religiously."

"We used to have a Christmas tree when the kids were little," Roslyn says. "But we stopped when we began going out of town for the holidays. I do put out the Christmas cards, for the seasonal aspect of it."

Because the Christian holiday of Christmas and the Jewish holiday of Hanukkah both take place in the month of December, conflicts may develop in the interfaith home. Some people call it the "December dilemma." Rabbi Stephen Hart says, "This is the time of year when differences are accentuated."

"This is the only time of year when you have to make a choice," says the mother of an interfaith family. "Sometimes you avoid it altogether by not having a Christmas tree or a Hanukkah menorah, by not making a statement."

Cheryl was raised Jewish in an interfaith family; her father is Christian. She married Patrick, a Christian who later converted to Judaism. "Even before Patrick converted, we never celebrated Christmas in this house," Cheryl says. "But we would go to my father's home and help decorate the tree. On Christmas morning, my son Jon would finish Hanukkah and then go to my dad's."

Jon likes to be with his grandparents when they celebrate Christmas. "I like to see what they do," he says. "I like to celebrate Christmas with my grandparents, but not here at home."

Patrick's mother sends Hanukkah presents, and his father sends Christmas presents. "But that's their choice. We never said this is what we want you to do," Patrick says.

Cheryl and Patrick do not have many Jewish neighbors, so they have a Hanukkah party and invite the children's friends from the neighborhood. The neighbors have ques-

tions: What do you do at a Hanukkah party? They serve
potato latkes (pancakes) and play games with a dreidel, a
four-sided top. "This gives our non-Jewish neighbors a
chance to share the holiday in the house with my children," Cheryl says. In turn, Cheryl and Patrick and their
family go to the home of Christian friends on Christmas
morning and share with them.

Although Lynn, who is Jewish, and Richard, who is
Lutheran, are raising their children Jewish, they celebrate Christmas. "That's the only Christian holiday we
celebrate in the house," Lynn says. "We have a Christmas
tree."

Lynn and Richard observe all the Jewish holidays. They
celebrate Christmas as well as Hanukkah, and their children, Kevin and Barry, get presents for both of them.
"That's what I like about it," Kevin says.

"When Hanukkah and Christmas overlap, Hanukkah
gets short shrift," Lynn says. "On Christmas day we don't
light the Hanukkah candles." Lynn and Richard often
celebrate with another interfaith family. They celebrate
Hanukkah at their house, and Christmas at the friends'
house.

Lynn had trouble with the first Christmas of her marriage. "We had to start small," she says. One Christmas,
when her sons were young, was especially hard for her. "I
thought that there was no way Hanukkah could possibly
compete with Christmas. How were we going to instill a
sense of pride in Judaism in the boys when there was
this thing called Christmas? Who wouldn't want to be
Christian, so you could have Christmas? I got myself in
such a state. And then I just decided that the best thing
to do was for us all to go down and have breakfast at
Marshall Field's department store under the big Christmas
tree. I decided to give in to it all.

"I still get very uncomfortable around the holidays because Christmas is a much more glamorous holiday than Hanukkah. Yes, it's fun, but it's very hard when you are trying to do things Jewishly to have to compete with Christmas."

Glenn and Melanie celebrate both Hanukkah and Christmas. They believe there is a secular, or non-religious, spirit that all can share. It is a time of giving. They have Christmas dinner and a Christmas tree. In Melanie's family, with their Baptist tradition, Christmas is a big celebration. "They do it in a big way," Melanie says. "It is an event for the family to come together."

Because of Glenn's Jewish background, it was difficult for him to participate in Christmas at first and to have a tree. Now he does. "I had to get over my own hangups," he says. Glenn has always appreciated how important Christmas is to Melanie. "It wouldn't be the same for Melanie without Christmas."

Teenagers Brent and Stacey have always had a Christmas tree and a Hanukkah menorah. "I didn't think about it," Brent says. "I just assumed most families did both, until I told my friends we're going to have a Christmas tree, and they were surprised."

Often, the choice of which holidays to celebrate and how to celebrate them is much more difficult for the parents than for the children in an interfaith family. To ten-year-old Barry, it is basic. "On Christmas, you just do things for Christmas, nothing for Hanukkah. On Hanukkah, you do nothing for Christmas."

"I'm glad you've made that distinction," Barry's mother, Lynn, responds. "I'm not always sure you understand that Hanukkah is our holiday, that it's simply not going to be as exciting as Christmas. But I think the family have really come to terms with the way we do things."

Renee says, "We used to have problems early in our marriage when we were still exploring our choices. We had an interfaith marriage, but we did not realize the differences in background. At first it was definitely a conflict. I was very nervous at Christmas, and Roger was very nervous at Hanukkah. It took a lot of exploration and giving and taking for a long time before we were comfortable with each other's holidays. Since we have children, we have chosen to be a Jewish family. Therefore, Hanukkah is emphasized more. At Christmas we don't have a tree; we have stockings. We try to de-emphasize Christmas."

"We exchange presents, have some wreaths and poinsettias," Roger says.

"Sometimes we get a lot of presents from Grandma," Russell adds. Roger's mother sends a big box of presents at Christmas.

"Renee is less berserk about Christmas time and having my identity not entirely wiped out," Roger says. "In time, we start trusting more and more. The kids get older, and it's not confusing to them."

The Hanukkah-Christmas dilemma is harder for Cheryl than for her children. "It's hard for me just to enjoy it," Cheryl says. "The children enjoy it because they are kids, and it's with the grandparents. They enjoy it on that level. There is so much more religious significance for me that it's harder."

On the other hand, it may be just as difficult for a Christian married to a non-Christian to give up the celebration of Christmas. A Christian woman married to a Jew said, "It means giving up things you grew up with. All I want is a Christmas tree!"

As an Islamic family, Elizabeth and Yosef and their children have never had a Christmas tree. Early in her marriage, and when her children were young, it was hard for Elizabeth—who was brought up in a Christian home—not to celebrate Christmas. "My children will never have the good memories, the family memories, of Christmas," Elizabeth says.

When Elizabeth's children were young, her parents sent them Christmas presents, and they sent presents to Elizabeth's parents. The children understood that Christmas was their grandparents' holiday and that it was very meaningful to them.

Some Muslim parents buy Christmas decorations but use them in Islamic celebrations. Because their family is in a predominantly Christian neighborhood, Elizabeth and Yosef feel that it is important to make Islamic holidays meaningful. Daud's Christian friend once complained, "Daud gets two *eids* [religious holidays when gifts are exchanged], and I only get one Christmas."

Children of interfaith families that celebrate both Christmas and Hanukkah often hear a similar complaint from their friends. "Maybe people are a little jealous that we have both," Stacey says. "They ask, 'How come you get to have a tree?' When I was a senior in high school, I had six friends over to help decorate our Christmas tree. They were all Jewish. Some of them had decorated a tree before, a Christian friend's tree, but they had never had a tree of their own."

To some Jews, celebrating Christmas is not a problem because they grew up regarding it as a nonreligious holiday. One Jewish man had a Christmas tree as a child but still felt Jewish. He thought of Christmas as an American holiday, not a religious one. "I don't want to deprive my own child of this holiday," he says.

For many interfaith families, whether or not to have a Christmas tree is the thorniest issue of all. "Every year, we discuss whether to get a tree, but we usually do get one," Marilyn says. "I haven't come to terms with the Christmas tree yet. I don't think we'll ever solve that problem."

Having a Christmas tree is not an issue for Debbie. "A tree is not really religion," she says.

Although Ray's family is Jewish, they have always celebrated both Christmas and Hanukkah. "When I was a child, my family always got their presents on Christmas," Ray says. "That's when we exchanged gifts. We never got Hanukkah presents, but we always got our presents Christmas morning. We did not have a tree or Christmas decorations, so we put the presents around the bottom of the piano. My family still does it that way."

Celebrating the religious holidays of both faiths can be physically as well as spiritually demanding. "It's a lot when December comes," Marilyn says. "Even earlier, when the fall comes and you start going from the High Holidays to Halloween to Thanksgiving. Then, depending when Hanukkah falls—sometimes it's early December, and sometimes it's exactly coordinated with Christmas—it seems as if you're celebrating something all the time. It's a never-ending thing. To me, that is a very negative aspect. It's a lot of preparation. We're doing Hanukkah dinner, and we're having Christmas dinner. When the children were little, we even had a play-group Christmas party! It just got to be too much."

Besides Christmas and Hanukkah, interfaith families mark many other holidays with family and friends.

When her son Zachary was younger, Karen started her own tradition for the Jewish High Holidays, Rosh Hashanah and Yom Kippur. "We kept Zachary out of school and went to the nature preserve near our home. My idea is that this is God's nature, and we're close to nature. It's the High Holy Days and we're not in temple, but we're together, and we're outside, and it's beautiful. So that became a tradition, a self-made tradition."

Before Karen's parents moved to her area, none of her family or Nick's family lived nearby. "We had some close friends who were Jewish, and they invited us over for the major Jewish holidays." After her parents moved to the area, Karen and Nick and their family had Passover seders, as well as Hanukkah, at her parents' house.

To share in his family's observance of Passover, Richard, a Protestant, likes to make gefilte fish, a traditional Jewish food. "When I go to the office, all my Jewish partners ask me how is my gefilte fish. They can smell me coming."

"I help to make the gefilte fish," Barry says. "One time, I was cutting the onions. The fumes were so strong, I couldn't see. Dad and I were both crying. It was a lot of fun."

Sometimes there is a conflict between Easter and Passover. "If we celebrated Easter during the eight days of Passover, I would not be able to eat everything. I can't eat any bread," Lynn says. Lynn and Richard go to Richard's mother's house to celebrate Easter. Because Richard's mother is now Russian Orthodox, the family celebrates the Christian Orthodox Easter, which never conflicts with Passover because it is based on the same calendar.

Celebrating religious holidays in the interfaith home may involve compromise. Rituals may have to be changed or modified. Traditionally the father or grandfather leads the Passover seder. "Because he's not Jewish, Richard cannot lead the seder," Lynn says. "So, if my father isn't with us, I lead the seder. Kevin will be able to when he is thirteen. There are other things that I've had to take over, things that the husband would do in the more typical Jewish household." Another way of compromising is to alternate holidays from one year to the next.

Many non-Christians can accept the secular holiday symbols such as a Christmas tree or an Easter basket but are offended by specific Christian symbols such as crosses. Interfaith families that do not observe the religious part of Easter enjoy coloring eggs and making Easter baskets. Glenn and Melanie's children go to a friend's home for an Easter egg hunt. However, a Catholic woman bringing up her children in the Jewish tradition says, "Families should have more than just the outward symbols of a religious holiday. They should observe the religiosity of the holiday as well."

Often, the attitudes and actions of the friends and relatives of the interfaith family can influence the success of the religious holidays. Planning family get-togethers is one way family and friends can work together for smooth celebration. A Jewish father says, "The family should maintain their religious identity in their own home, but it is good to share the holidays of others outside of the home. You can share holidays with the Christian grandparents."

Family get-togethers are an important part of many religious holidays. They are an opportunity to share the various religious traditions of the interfaith family. Marilyn's children have gone to family get-togethers since they were babies. "The baby bottle goes to the Passover seder," she says.

To fifteen-year-old Josh, the family's getting together is more significant than the religious meaning of the holidays. "I have been exposed to the holidays on my father's side of the family, Rosh Hashanah and Passover," Josh says. "But I think of it more as going to Uncle Dave's and Aunt Nora's for dinner and seeing family members you haven't seen for a year. I don't really believe in the religious sense that goes along with it."

Although Elena and her sons are Catholic, they celebrate the Jewish holidays with Ray's family. Elena says, "When the boys were very young, before we could travel, we had Passover. I would make a seder and go to great lengths to make it kosher. As the boys grew older, we would have seders with the Jewish aunts and uncles, and the boys participated. I also had candles on Hanukkah and Friday night, and I tried to make Jewish dishes."

"That was a very nice accommodation, something you didn't have to do," Ray says.

"It meant as much to Ray as it did to me," Elena continues. "I felt it was important to keep this tradition. As the children grow and life gets busy, it's hard to keep one tradition, let alone two, in the busyness of life."

Conversely, Elena's Jewish sister-in-law gets in the spirit of Elena's holidays. "Every Christmas since I can remember, Ray's sister has made our boys a Christmas ornament," Elena says. "Ray's family doesn't have Christmas trees or lights or any observance of that sort, but every year his sister makes the boys a beautiful ornament."

Claudia and Eric have felt no pressure from either his or her parents about holiday celebrations. "We realize it is important for us to go to church as a family on the holidays, whether it's the Catholic church or the Protestant church," Claudia says.

In other cases, pressures from family or friends can be the cause of problems associated with holiday observance. "From time to time when we were first married, I felt pressure from Richard's mother," Lynn says. "One year she gave me a Christmas tree ornament. She just assumed we would have a Christmas tree. I had a real hard time with that. We hadn't made that decision yet."

When Karen and Nick were first married, their biggest problem with religious holidays was learning each other's customs. "I did wonder how other people might react to the way we were doing things," Karen says. Karen's Jewish father could not accept their celebrating Christmas. Karen planned on having her father come to visit in December. "We had a Christmas tree with a Jewish star on top. I was really proud of it. But my father was very uneasy. He made an excuse not to come after all so he wouldn't have to deal with it."

Some parents set restrictions on how the holidays are celebrated, or what grandparents or friends can do. Patrick says, "We restrict only what we do in the house. We celebrate only the Jewish holidays in the house, but outside we go by whosever house we are in."

Even at a very young age, a child may understand that there are different religions and different observances. When Cheryl's son Jon was in preschool, Cheryl was an assistant teacher. The teachers' center was in a Catholic girls' school. Cheryl was taking something down to be laminated, near the kitchen. It was Christmas time, and nuns in full habit were making cookies. While Jon waited for his mother, a nun gave him a Christmas cookie and asked, "What do you want for Christmas?"

"We don't celebrate Christmas," Jon answered.

"Oh, what do you celebrate?"

"We celebrate Hanukkah. What do you celebrate?"

"We celebrate Christmas," the nun responded.

Jon thought for a moment. "That's okay," he said, "because we both believe in God."

Later Cheryl said, "Somehow Jon made us think, what difference does it make?"

No matter how an interfaith family chooses to celebrate them, the religious holidays are a significant part of family life. As one father said: "The most important part of the holidays is family togetherness and loving, warm feelings."

CHAPTER ◇ 7

Sharing Religious Experiences

Nick stood at the hospital's nursery window and looked at his newborn son, Zachary. Nick, from a Catholic family, and his wife Karen, who is Jewish, had already decided to raise their son in both religions.

Zachary was only two hours old, but Nick knew it was time for a very important event in Zachary's life. Nick turned and asked a passing nurse for a glass of water.

"Are you going to faint?" the nurse asked.

"No," Nick said, "I'm going to baptize my son."

"Oh, how nice," the nurse said, "nobody has ever done that on my shift before."

With the water, Nick made the sign of the cross over Zachary's head and said, "I baptize you in the name of the Father and the Son and the Holy Spirit."

"I like the fact that you did that," Karen says. "It was almost like your participation in the birth."

"I figure Zachary is covered," Nick says. "Because, according to Judaism, if the mother is Jewish, the child is Jewish, too. And now that Zachary has been baptized, he can travel in either religion. It was comforting to me to do that."

"Nick's mother did that with all her children," Karen says. "For me, it was like carrying on a family tradition. We had already established that it was important."

Religious life-cycle events such as baptism, confirmation, and bar or bat mitzvah may be important and even essential events in any family. However, because each of these occasions tends to strengthen the bonds people feel toward their own religion, they can create problems in the interfaith family.

The issue of baptism may bring an early conflict, especially when a Catholic is married to a non-Catholic. "We Catholics are taught from the first stage of catechism that if you're not baptized, you're damned," Nick says. "So you have to be baptized. I carry enough of that belief with me, that it is essential for a child to be baptized first thing. That is why I baptized my son."

In the Catholic-Protestant family, if the churches of both partners have infant baptism, one parent may feel the child is being excluded from his or her church when the child is baptized in the other parent's church. Conflicts may also arise if one partner believes in infant baptism and the other believes in adult baptism.

Author Richard Lawless suggests that, to ease these difficulties, the parents may add to an infant baptism a "welcoming" ceremony into the partner's church; or clergy from both of the parents' traditions could baptize the child. One interfaith couple incorporated aspects of both Judaism and Catholicism when their baby was christened. Another couple used a priest and a rabbi.

Claudia, from a Protestant family, says her parents were not happy when her children were baptized Catholic. However, because her husband is Catholic, Claudia felt obligated to have her children baptized in the Catholic Church.

Claudia's oldest son, Peter, was three months old when he was baptized. "I wasn't really happy about this," Claudia says. "I felt like I was giving my son over to someone else." Because of her uneasiness, Claudia asked her own minister to be present at the baptism. Usually, in the Catholic church, several infants are baptized at a special service on a Sunday afternoon. In Claudia's Congregational Church, baptism is part of the regular Sunday morning service.

On the afternoon of Peter's baptism, Claudia's minister went with her to the service. Having no idea what to expect, he wore his minister's robe, prepared to say something and be part of the service. "There we all were, several sets of parents with crying babies, and this one very tall minister in a robe standing there and not knowing what to do. And me, very nervous and very uncomfortable," Claudia recalls. "I wasn't quite prepared for it, but it ended up being very funny. My minister just hung around, waiting to go through the ritual of these people, and they were all looking at him and wondering, 'What are you doing here?'"

"When our sons were baptized, we kept a very low profile," Elena says. "I thought it was something that might hurt Ray's mother, and I didn't want to make a big thing out of it. So we had very low-key baptisms, as well as first communions and other events. We didn't have big parties. Because Ray's family lives out of town, it is easier to do things that way. It would have been hard to have a first communion with Ray's family in town and not invite them. And I wouldn't have invited them. It would have made it much stickier."

Many churches expect young teens to be confirmed or have an adult baptism. These ceremonies mark the beginning of a person's acceptance of, and responsibility for, his own faith. However, they can cause problems in the Catholic-Protestant or Christian-Jewish family because they seem to establish that the young person now belongs to the tradition of just one parent.

In the Jewish religion, bar mitzvah or bat mitzvah is also a time when young people accept responsibility for their own faith. Many families who are raising their children Jewish expect their sons and daughters to be bar or bat mitzvahed. Others do not.

When Annie was bat mitzvahed, she drew from her father's Jewish heritage and her mother's Chinese heritage. Her bat mitzvah in the synagogue was followed by lunch in a Chinese restaurant. Annie's bat mitzvah was a big day for the family, a very important event. Her Christian grandparents attended happily and were very accepting.

Debbie, a Jew married to a Protestant, made a different decision. "We decided not to have bar mitzvah or bat mitzvah," she says. "Although we gave the children the option, I was not big on the idea. Too many people do it so they can say they did it and have a big party, and then they quit. In my opinion, if you're really committed to your religion, you stay on until you are confirmed."

Marilyn says, "I never had a bat mitzvah, and I'm not that committed to Judaism. I don't want to give that investment of time to Hebrew school. I don't want to get involved in it. I see how bar mitzvahs are done, so lavish, and I don't want to get caught up in that whole thing. I think my sons can be very happily Jewish—or not Jewish, if they choose—when they grow up without having a bar mitzvah."

"At one time Josh wanted to learn Hebrew, and at one point he was considering whether to be bar mitzvahed," Sandy says. "We had a talk about it. It isn't just a matter of learning your part to be bar mitzvahed; it is a matter of making a commitment to a whole system of beliefs. When Josh really thought about it, he did learn Hebrew, but he pretty quickly decided that he was interested in learning but not ready to make the commitment.

In the interfaith family, as in the same-faith family, parents must make decisions about the religious education of their children, as well as what life-cycle events to observe. When Annie began wondering about God, her parents decided it was time for her to start religious school. But the decision was left up to Annie, and she chose to go. Annie's Jewish grandfather paid the school expenses to get the children started. Annie says, "I had a choice to go to Hebrew school. But once I had chosen to go, my brother Scott had to go, too."

Their mother, Melanie, did not receive religious training in her Baptist background, and she missed it. "I want my children to be grounded in their religion," she says.

"When I was going into the eighth grade, my parents gave me the choice," Stacey says. "I could continue with my Jewish education or stop and be whatever I wanted to be. I decided to continue with my education."

"You received the religious education. Now it's your

choice to accept it or reject it," says Stacey's father, Mitch. Her mother, Debbie, says, "We thought it was a good idea to send our children to religious school because it's not good to grow up only knowing about soccer and cars. You need to have something to be part of."

In Claudia and Eric's Protestant-Catholic family, their three sons have been going to Sunday school since they were two or three years old. "We have followed a pattern; up until second grade the children go to the Protestant Sunday school," Claudia says. "In second grade, they start the religious education program at the Catholic church. Because they have first communion in the second grade, the children have to switch then if they want to have it. Peter is the only one who has had his first communion. He just kept on going to the Catholic church. Soon his brothers, David and James, will switch over. I don't know whether Peter will come back to the Protestant church.

"There were no problems switching from the Protestant to the Catholic church. Peter's teacher was a friend of ours, so I felt very comfortable about that. Peter didn't have any problem with it, either. I think, if anything, he may prefer the Catholic Sunday school because kids from school go there."

In an interfaith family where one parent is Catholic, deciding whether to send the children to Catholic school can become an issue. Claudia and Eric do not send their sons to Catholic school. "I am more comfortable having them go to the Catholic Sunday school for their Catholic religious education, than I would be if they went to the Catholic school," Claudia says.

Elena and Ray also agreed on this issue before marriage. "Part of our prenuptial agreement was that our children would never go to Catholic school," Elena says.

"It just happens that in this area, both the public and

the Catholic schools are excellent," Ray says. "So the choice was not between sending them to a good Catholic school or a rotten public school or vice versa."

For most of their school years, Elena and Ray's three sons attended public school as well as Catholic Sunday school. "From kindergarten all through school, our sons went to Sunday school, except for the two years we lived in England," Elena explains. "When we lived there, we discovered an excellent prep school in walking distance from our home. It happened to be the Irish Christian Brothers school, a Catholic school. It was a much better school than the public schools in our neighborhood.

"When we returned here, the boys went to public school, and they had the Catholic Sunday school program and the youth group. I also hired a tutor, because I considered this program ineffectual for teaching the boys about their faith. Through a Jesuit priest friend, I found a tutor who teaches at a very conservative Catholic school. He came here and tutored the boys once a week."

Cheryl's children attend Jewish religious school, and Cheryl teaches there. "At least half of the children in my class are from interfaith families," Cheryl says. "Most are children of teachers at school. All of the parents are still non-Jewish, in most cases Jewish mothers and non-Jewish fathers. On parents' day, some non-Jewish parents appear very uncomfortable in the religious school environment."

When Cheryl teaches, her approach to her class is influenced by her own upbringing in an interfaith family. "I'm conscious of the fact that when I talk to my class, we come to it differently. Everybody has different traditions at home." When interfaith children attend religious school, they may become more aware of the religious differences between their parents.

Marilyn also is a religious school teacher. She has

observed that some of the children have no knowledge of Judaism. "Not only the children from interfaith families, but those with two Jewish parents, as well. I don't have problems or make adjustments in the curriculum related to interfaith children, although our synagogue has quite a lot of them."

Lynn, who teaches in a Jewish religious school, tells about one young boy from an interfaith family. "He is very confused," Lynn says. "He constantly brings up things about Christianity and Christian holidays that are very inappropriate to what we are talking about. It's confusing to the younger children. With the older children I sometimes have to discuss that it is okay to celebrate both Christian and Jewish holidays. That doesn't make you weird or abnormal; you don't have to apologize."

Children from interfaith homes may have different attitudes or perceptions about topics that come up in religious school. For instance, Marilyn's class was talking about Jews in 15th-century Spain who had to observe their religion in secret; they would have been executed if they were discovered to be Jews. Marilyn asked the class, "What would you do, convert, be a secret Jew, or die?"

"Half of the children—those from interfaith homes— said they would convert without hesitation," Marilyn says. "They think, my mother or father is not Jewish. This is an interfaith perception. It is not something alien to them."

Rabbi Stephen Hart says that interfaith families have an influence on Jewish religious schools. "By the year 2000," Rabbi Hart predicts, "half of the students in our Reform religious schools will have one parent who is not Jewish. We must consider how that impacts on our teaching, what we teach, and how we teach. What kind of knowledge should our faculty have? What kind of sensitivity do our teachers need? When we used to teach about *Shabbat*, we would say, 'Dad did the kiddush [prayer over the wine], and Mom lit the candles.' When Mom is not Jewish, is it appropriate for her to do that, and how does she do it? There is a variety of issues here, and teachers need guidelines on how to address all the issues created by the increasing number of interfaith families." Handbooks and study plans are being developed as resources for religious schools.

In Michelle and Gary's Buddhist family, their children attend Sunday classes at the Buddhist temple. Their son Brad earned a Cub Scout award by studying with the minister.

"We didn't really have formal religious training for our children," says Roslyn, a Jewish woman married to a Hindu. But they were exposed to everything and went to all kinds of temples, Indian temples, and synagogues.

"When Lisa was nursery school age, I sent her to the Jewish Community Center nursery school. There they observed the sabbath on Friday and lit the candles. I thought in the beginning that it would be a good idea to give Lisa some background in her Jewish heritage. But she was coming home and telling us, you have to do this, you have to do that, becoming very dogmatic about it. I didn't want there to be a difference between her and her father. So I decided that formal religious education would not a good idea in our situation.

"Sometimes I wonder if we should have given the children formal religious training so in time of need they could turn to religion. But I feel that young children don't turn to religion for help; they turn to people, teachers, parents, or friends. The formalized religion brings out more differences in relationships than it brings people together."

Sometimes interfaith parents provide for their children's religious education at home. This is what Karen and Nick did. "We've been more active in Zachary's religious education in the past year," Karen says. "I've gotten some children's books."

"Since Karen and I have religious training as part of our lives, we're okay religiously," Nick adds. "We don't know if the training we're giving Zachary is going to benefit him. We won't know that for a while. If he comes up without the necessary resources, if he is lacking in the skills to help him survive because of a lack of religious training, then we've failed. That's the long term.

"What Zachary is getting religiously is far behind what other children his age are getting in specific religions. Boys of his age are studying for bar mitzvah, and Catholic boys have had first communion and confirmation. He's behind because we wanted to wait until he was old enough before giving him that information. In Catholicism, they don't care whether you understand or not. They just tell you and expect you to repeat it back to them. We wanted to wait to be sure there was some understanding on Zachary's part."

Interfaith parents may want their children to learn about their cultural or ethnic heritage, as well as their religious heritage. Yosef took his wife and children—who were born in the United States—to Saudi Arabia to give them the experience of living in an Islamic environment. They were able to experience the Islamic call to prayer and to participate in *hajj*, the pilgrimage of Muslims to Mecca.

Having their children receive a religious education, along with the rituals that accompany that education, is important to many interfaith families. It is also important to them that the family attend religious services in the synagogue, church, mosque, or temple.

. "Richard is very supportive when there are family services at the synagogue," Lynn says. "He goes with us. He goes with me for the High Holidays. He's involved to the extent he can be without being Jewish himself, participating with the family and as a husband."

Michelle, who was brought up as a Buddhist, says her parents are very proud to have the grandchildren so actively involved in the Buddhist temple with their friends and friends' children. "Our family is much more involved and active than they had been in the past," she says.

Other interfaith families are less involved in religious activities, or disinterested. "I no longer go to the synagogue," Sandy says. "Josh and Carly sometimes go with their dad if there's a holiday; but we don't belong. The other complicating thing is that the children's step-father is not Jewish; he's Protestant."

Josh was seven and his sister Carly was four when their parents were divorced. "It's gotten to the point with me that I don't care to go to the synagogue much anymore," Josh says. "Sometimes I go if it will make Dad feel better, relieve some tension in his life. But I don't go for myself."

Some families attend services in the house of worship of each parent. Lynn and Richard and their sons attend religious services together. They go to the synagogue on occasion, especially the High Holidays. They have also attended Christmas Eve services in Richard's church. In another interfaith family, Roger remains Christian, but he does not attend church regularly. He goes to the synagogue with his family more often than to church.

"When we visit Mitch's parents in Iowa, we go to church with them," Debbie says. "Here, we go to High Holiday services."

Protestant-Catholic couples may go to each other's services. Some alternate Sundays. Others go separately on most Sundays, but use Christmas, family celebrations, and other special times to go together to both churches. "Occasionally, we all go to church together," Eric says. "Claudia goes to the Catholic church more often than I go to the Protestant church. But there is no big planned program." Claudia adds, "For example, we go to Christmas Eve mass instead of a service at my church, because the Catholic church is closer. It fits into our Christmas Eve plans a lot better."

Elena goes to High Holiday services in the synagogue with Ray. Occasionally, their Catholic-raised sons go with them. The family go to church on Christmas and Easter. Ray's parents and brothers are observant Jews. They go to Friday night services. His brother is president of the synagogue and is actively involved, even though he also is intermarried.

"Zachary has been to synagogue and church," Karen says. "We are fairly casual about our religions. We don't go to church or synagogue on a regular weekly basis. We're traditionalists in the sense that we like the religious traditions, especially where family is involved. Family is important, so the religious traditions that go along with family are very important." Although Karen was brought up in a Jewish home, she appreciates the spiritual feelings her husband Nick has in his Catholic services. "When we go to church on Good Friday, I think the whole story of Good Friday and Easter Sunday is beautiful. I can get emotional about it, not necessarily religiously. And I detect emotion in Nick. I wonder, when Zachary gets older, will he feel emotional ties to either of our religions. Will he be inclined to go and worship?"

If a family attend religious services and send the children to religious school, the choice of a house of worship is important. Many factors influence an interfaith family's choice, including the attitude of the religious leadership toward interfaith families, and even location.

Often, interfaith families choose a house of worship where they feel most welcome. That was the case with Lynn and Richard. "It's more than just choosing a synagogue," Lynn says. "It's the rabbi. Our rabbi is very liberal."

Richard says, "At one of the High Holiday services, the rabbi suggested that people be like Christians in some respects. I think that statement was for the benefit of some of us non-Jewish members in the audience."

"I think people are very ecumenical," Lynn responds. "But that's what makes it comfortable for us and our family at that synagogue."

Because of the growing numbers of interfaith families who join Reform Jewish synagogues, these congregations are now discussing the role of the non-Jew in the life of the synagogue. "We have many non-Jews who not only find themselves amidst the congregation, but who choose to become involved in the life of the congregation," says Rabbi Hart. Questions come up as to the propriety of the non-Jew's participation. Can such persons serve on committees or the board of trustees? Can they participate in religious services? "It is these kinds of questions that years ago people did not pay much attention to and are now becoming increasingly important."

For an interfaith family to be happy with a house of

worship, the rabbis, teachers, and staff must be sensitive to the feelings of both parents. When Annie was preparing for her bat mitzvah, her mother Melanie phoned the synagogue office to ask about the lunch following the service. "What shall I serve?" she asked.

"The usual things," was the reply.

Melanie was Chinese with a Baptist upbringing. Bat mitzvahs and the lunches following them were not part of her heritage. "What are the usual things?" she asked.

"Oh, you know, the usual things."

Melanie could not get a more helpful reply. "The synagogue was very uncooperative. They expected me to know the rules," Melanie says. So, instead of a lunch at the synagogue, she planned a lunch at a Chinese restaurant.

Some couples may "try out" different houses of worship, even those of different religions. "We've found a church that we like," Karen says. "There is a synagogue nearby that is very accepting of interfaith couples. Another synagogue was not very open. I didn't check them out because I didn't want to be put in the position of not being accepted. A couple I know didn't feel comfortable there."

Occasionally, a church or synagogue is chosen for practical rather than philosophical reasons. Debbie says, "I grew up as a Conservative Jew. We weren't going to do that, considering we had two different religions, so we went to Reform Judaism. Then that synagogue moved; it was too far to drive in the winter. We looked for a synagogue around here, and we joined Humanistic Judaism. Actually, we didn't believe completely in its philosophy, but we believed in part of it. We liked the rabbi a lot. We went to the service, and Mitch said he really liked the man and his ideas. You could believe in

God and everything else, and still believe in yourself. I think that's what my daughter liked about the rabbi. She stayed in religious school a couple more years to be in his class and learn more about his ideas. He was a really good teacher."

"You pick a church because it is in the area," Eric says. "Especially with the Catholic Church, you usually go to the church in the parish. Probably more often than the Protestants, you don't really choose the church you go to." After they were married, Claudia continued to go to the church she had attended for many years, even though it was in another suburb.

"Deciding on joining a synagogue and choosing one was a problem that didn't have an easy resolution," Marilyn says. "Until our son Steven was about seven, we didn't acknowledge the problem. Many synagogues in our area are hard to get into. They have long waiting lists, and they're expensive. So we just went round and round. Once we decided we would have a Jewish home, it was hard to carry it out. We finally joined the synagogue that offered me a teaching position. It became the entry for all of us and for the children into religious school. It was very close to home, and the people were very nice. It just seemed to work out."

"Our family has attended services in a wide variety of synagogues and temples, mostly of the Eastern religions," Roslyn says. "We go to Hindu temples, Sikh and Jain temples. Before the temples were built, which was fairly recently, people had services in their homes, one Sunday a month. Families took turns having services, both in the Sikh and the Hindu. People felt that it was a blessing to have it in their home.

"Our children were exposed to a variety of cultures that way. They were exposed more to Hindu types of ceremonies than to Jewish or other Western religious rites. We would go to the blessing of a house, where a religious person says prayers to bless the house. Also, we have attended ceremonies to bless a baby, for good luck, or to thank God for favors granted. Most of the Hindu services take place in people's homes."

One parent may become quite active in the religion of the other parent. For instance, a Christian father might tutor in the Jewish religious school. Reform Rabbi Harold Kudan has said that for Judaism to survive, Jews have to accept the idea that non-Jews can practice Jewish traditions.

Roger agrees. "If they had shut me out, we might have split up," he says. Now Roger is not only accepted by the congregation but very involved in it. "I am able to experience religion with my family, and we have all benefited."

Roger and Renee believe that it is important for the partner of the "other religion" to feel comfortable, even welcome, in the house of worship of the dominant religion. At one time, they belonged to a synagogue that they describe as "very uppity, with a rabbi who was neither warm nor spiritual." Renee was teaching kindergarten in the religious school. One family day, Roger was teasing the rabbi. "If you need any teachers, I might be available."

Roger's daughter, Rebecca, said in a loud voice, "Daddy you can't teach, you're Christian!" Everyone in the room was silent, looking at the rabbi.

"Instead of being a good sport, the rabbi turned beet red and just turned around and left the room," Roger recalls.

When choosing a house of worship, the feelings of the parent of the "other religion" must be taken into account.

"It depends a lot on how I am received," Roger says. "We have lived in several places, and in some synagogues I have not felt comfortable at all, but out of place and somewhat of an outcast. One of the reasons we moved back here is that I am accepted like anyone else in the synagogue. It has been really enjoyable and wonderful for me, because now our family is experiencing religion together in the broad sense.

"To me it makes all the difference in the world. I never really had a problem with the religious aspects of Judaism versus Christianity. But it makes a big difference how the congregation receives you. I'm very involved and have enjoyed it and enjoyed the experience. I think the kids have benefited from it. I certainly have. We have all benefitted.

"Just doing things: going to synagogue, going to family worship, being a spiritual unit, that is what I like. I had thought I would have to give up any religious bonding with my family. Now I feel there's a real chance to be together at the synagogue. And, because the synagogue is so accepting, I can get more out of the religious aspect. I have a chance to share a religious experience with my kids."

CHAPTER 8

A Personal Decision: Conversion

P atrick, Cheryl, and their four-year-old son, Jon, were driving to the home of Patrick's father for a birthday party. Jon was usually excited about seeing his grandfather, but today he was very quiet in the back seat. Cheryl asked, "Is something the matter?"

Jon looked out the window and then at his mother. "I'm confused," he said. "If you are Jewish, and Dad is Jewish, and I am Jewish, why isn't Grandpa Jewish?"

Cheryl smiled and explained to Jon that, although his dad had been born a Christian, he had decided to convert to Judaism the same year that Jon was born.

"Is Grandpa still going to be my Grandpa?" Jon asked.

"Of course, he's always going to be your grandpa," Cheryl told Jon. "He celebrates different holidays in his house, and we celebrate with him. But we choose not to celebrate those holidays in our house."

*   *   *

Conversion—where one partner converts to the religion of the other—is often a topic of discussion in an interfaith relationship. Some partners convert to the religion of the other partner before marriage. Others do not make the decision until after marriage, some waiting for many years until after they have children. Some people refuse to convert and never do.

People consider conversion for a variety of reasons. Some come to feel more comfortable with the religious beliefs of their partner than with the religion they were born into. Others convert to create unity and harmony in the marriage or to prevent some of the problems that occur in mixed marriages. Some parents convert so that their children can grow up in a household with just one religion. Still others feel forced into conversion by family members or by religious leaders.

With the changes in attitudes toward mixed marriage has come a change in attitude toward the need for conversion. Thirty or more years ago, greater pressure was placed on one partner to convert to the religion of the other.

According to author Dean Hoge, in about half of Catholic-Protestant marriages, one partner converts. The division is even between Catholic-to-Protestant and Protestant-to-Catholic conversions. The other half of the marriages remain mixed. In a Protestant-Catholic marriage, conversion usually takes place near the time of the wedding or before the first child is ten years old. "Intermarriage between Catholics and Protestants is the greatest single source of new Catholic converts," Hoge says.

Egan Mayer reports that the rate of conversion of non-Jewish spouses to Judaism has kept pace with the rapidly rising rate of intermarriage, so that the proportion of converts has remained constant. The 1990 National Jewish Population Survey reveals that, because of the conversion of many women before or after their marriage to Jews, two thirds of the Jews By Choice (converted Jews) are female.

A person's decision to convert or not to convert can affect the religious identity of the children. In families where the non-Jewish parent converts to Judaism, the children are much more likely to identify as Jews than those in homes where the non-Jewish parent does not convert, Mayer reports.

The desire to convert may be a natural result of an inter-faith relationship. When one person has a close relationship with someone of a different faith, that person may come to understand and accept the other faith and want to be a part of it. Conversion may not have been the original idea, but it develops to that point.

Patrick was the son of an Episcopalian minister. He married Cheryl, a Jew. Even before they were married, Patrick agreed that their children would be raised Jewish, but at that time he did not consider converting. Deciding to convert was a slow process. Married to Cheryl, Patrick was exposed to Judaism and Jewish traditions for many years. Cheryl taught religious school and was active in the Jewish community.

"It began to seem likely that I would convert," Patrick says. "After my son Jon was born, I woke up one day and said, 'This is my decision.'"

When Patrick told his father, the reaction was, "I wish it had been the other way. I wish Cheryl had converted to Christianity. But it is better for the children to have just one religion in the household."

Cheryl wrote to her mother-in-law in Texas. As the wife of a minister, Patrick's mother was very much involved in the church. "I wanted her to understand that this was something Patrick had done," Cheryl says, "that I had not asked him to do it. I understood that it must be hard for her. It would have been hard for my family if it had gone the other way. I wanted her to know that our children were still her grandchildren."

In another situation, Elizabeth made her decision to convert from Christianity to Islam just before her marriage to Yosef. "I had questions that Islam answered," Elizabeth says. "Yosef was influential in my acceptance of his religion." She declared her acceptance of Islam minutes before the wedding ceremony.

Elizabeth never discussed with her parents her intention to convert to Islam. "I showed them through my beliefs and my actions," she says. Elizabeth's parents approved of her decision because they had always wanted her and her sister to be independent and to think for themselves. They told Elizabeth that they accepted her decision because it was what "was good for you."

Eileen, a Christian married to a Jew, says, "I was brought up Unitarian. My argument had always been, I can have a Jewish household, I don't need to convert. I feel comfortable with everything. Why do I need to convert when I can have a Jewish home without it? I felt that Mark had accepted me for who I was, and not for what I was or wasn't.

"But when I started to consider having children, my thinking began to change. It took five years. Then I could start looking at the issue more rationally, without all the emotion. I was sort of teetering on whether to convert or not. I felt that now that we were having children, I was going to have a Jewish home, and I was going to participate in the Jewish community. Because the woman has the most influence with the children, I felt that I could best do that by converting."

It is often said that the convert is more devout than the partner who grew up in that faith. One woman converting to Judaism says she is making her husband's family more Jewish. Under her influence, his family will have its first Passover seder this year.

Five years after her marriage, Lila converted from Christianity to Judaism. She says she is "more Jewish" than her husband, who was born Jewish. She does not consider their family to be an interfaith family, but a Jewish one. The children are being raised Jewish. She always planned it that way. There was no family conflict. "My parents have accepted my decision, although they may not understand why I made that decision," Lila says.

In some families, neither partner chooses to convert. They may not feel it is necessary for family harmony, or they may each want to maintain their own faith. Larry, a Christian married to a Jewish woman, saw no need to convert because he was never very religious in the first place. "It's kind of like inertia," he says. "There was never any religion, so why should I start now?"

Tom, a Catholic married to a Jew, is raising his children in a Jewish household. However, he is not considering converting. "Conversion by me is as likely to occur as an earthquake under our house," Tom says with a laugh.

Melanie, a Chinese woman brought up as a Christian and now married to a Jew, saw no need to convert. "My Chinese ethnicity is all-encompassing. It is your identity; it's what you are. You can't convert out of Chinese."

"It's the same for Jews," Melanie's husband, Glenn,

adds. "Even when Jews convert, they are still considered Jewish by other Jews."

Richard, a Christian married to a Jew, is not thinking about converting to Judaism. "I go to Jewish religious services once in a while, and it's not what I expect out of a religious occasion," Richard says. "The Jewish service is different. The Lutheran church I went to was very traditional, and that's what I'm most comfortable with. I already have a church; I don't need a second one."

Roger, also a Protestant married to a Jew, does not feel a need to convert to Judaism. He does not want to give up his own religious heritage. "Our synagogue and rabbi are very accepting of who he is," Roger's wife, Renee, says. "They don't put pressure on him to convert."

Ray, a Jew married to a Catholic, never felt any pressure to convert. "Before I married Elena, I made it clear to her and her family that conversion was a nonstarter," Ray says. "There wasn't a spark of possibility. Never." Elena says, "My mother would be scandalized when my brothers would talk against the Catholic Church in front of Ray, because she thought they were spoiling any possibility of his converting. She just didn't understand that there *was* no possibility."

When Claudia, a Protestant, was planning to marry Eric, a Catholic, she was surprised to learn that her own grandmother was upset that she wasn't converting to Catholicism. Two of her grandmother's daughters had converted when they married Catholics. "This was an earlier time," Claudia explains. "They had to convert in order to get married. It would have been fine with my grandmother if Eric became a non-Catholic or if I became a Catholic. The important thing to her was that we should be together, we should have the same religion. Right now, we are happy with the way things are, sharing our two religions with our three sons. Conversion is not a consideration for me, not seriously. It crosses my mind when I'm disappointed in things going on in my church, but I don't think I ever will convert."

Some people do not wish to convert but feel pressured into doing so by their in-laws. Sandy, who was raised as a Catholic in an interfaith home, says, "When I was pregnant with my first child, Daniel's relatives were determined that I convert. They were Orthodox Jews. I was adamant that I not convert. Still, I ended up going through an Orthodox conversion, which left me with nothing but anger. I felt no need to convert. I had already agreed to raise our children in a Jewish home. Daniel himself didn't practice anything near Orthodox Jewish customs. That was a bad beginning.

"I married Daniel without converting. But I felt incredibly pressured. It just seemed like I was making so many people unhappy. I knew then that I should not go through with the conversion, and I should have listened to myself."

Roslyn, a Jew, and her husband, Lee, who is Hindu, object to the pressures people put on them and their children to convert. "We once took Lisa and her brother to a Passover seder, and someone tried to persuade our son to convert," Roslyn reports. "We said that was the last time we would attend a seder."

Lee says, "When I was a college student here in the United States, I knew a Catholic family. They wanted to convert me. I said, 'Fine, if it makes you happy.' But when the day came, I had one question: What am I converting from and to what? It makes you happy, so I am doing it out of respect for you. My feelings inside are feelings for you, not for any God. I am still the son of my parents, and I still have my brothers and sisters whom I respect. They said that my soul would be protected, so there was satisfaction in the converting and not for the one being converted. I did not find that satisfaction in my mind. If it makes you happy, you can call me Catholic. But my name is not changed, my blood is not different, my face is not changed, my parents are not different.

"The word conversion is a Western word. It has nothing to do with Eastern culture. How can you convert? You can't convert to something else; then you are denying everything that you were. It's like saying that what I was, I don't like; now I'm something else, a new person. If I ask someone to convert, that's an insult; I am asking her to forget her background, what she was brought up with. I married my wife with her background. I didn't want her to become such a strong Hindu that she had to reject Judaism."

"My husband once asked me to convert, and we almost broke up about it," Lisa says. "I told him, you're not accepting what I am, you're asking me to change my beliefs just because you came into my life."

Even when people choose to convert, not all problems are solved. "Although I converted from Christianity to Judaism five years ago, I still have issues to resolve," Cindy says. "It is still hard for me to talk to my parents about my new Jewish life. I still color Easter eggs. After all, I still have my Christian background."

Before Vatican Council II in 1965, Catholics who married non-Catholics had to promise that they would strive for the conversion of their spouses. This is no longer true. The Catholic Church today views conversion as a personal choice and does not pressure the non-Catholic partner to convert.

In pre-Cana classes for Catholics preparing to marry, conversion is not a goal. "But it may be a side effect," says Frank Hannigan. "Priests conduct the pre-Cana classes. During the course of the classes, a couple may come up to the priest and say that one is ready to convert. They are comfortable with that priest."

The process of converting to Catholicism is called the Rite of Christian Initiation. It once was part of the catechism, or moral and religious instruction. "Today, the approach is more holistic," explains Father Michael Place. In an endeavor to learn about the whole of the religion, the person interested in converting begins with exploring the structure of Catholicism. Then, if the person chooses, he or she moves on to in-depth study. Depending on the parish, the program takes six to twelve months to complete. It culminates on Holy Saturday (Easter Eve), the Easter Vigil, with baptism and the first Eucharist.

"One should not convert just to get married," Father Place says. If, right before marriage, a person is ready to convert, he should do it before getting married. "If you are not at that point, don't convert before marriage. Attend church with your Catholic spouse, and if your interest grows into faith, then convert."

In the Christian Orthodox church, a non-Orthodox is not obliged to convert. However, the Orthodox partner is informed of the consequences of marrying a non-Orthodox, such as losing standing in the Church. To convert to Christian Orthodox, a non-Christian is given catechism, a period of instruction set by the priest. He or she is then baptized and confirmed. The process is the same for Christians, except that they do not have to be baptized; their baptism is accepted.

*   *   *

The exact details of the process of conversion to Protestantism vary from one denomination to another. The primary step is baptism if the person has not already been baptized. If the person has been baptized, he or she is confirmed.

"Conversion requires education and spiritual growth," says Protestant minister Donna Gray. "A person believes in Jesus Christ as the Savior, trusts in Him, and wants to be His disciple. The person would be educated as to what that means. The person would become a confirmed member of the church, and this also would require education. Catholics can convert to Protestantism. They don't need to be rebaptized. They are taken in as church members. Before the congregation, they pledge to support the church."

In Orthodox and Conservative Judaism, a person with a Jewish mother is considered Jewish. One with a Jewish father and a non-Jewish mother is not Jewish and would have to convert to Judaism to be considered Jewish. Reform Judaism recognizes patrilineal descent, accepting a person as Jewish without conversion if either the mother or the father is Jewish and if the person was raised as a Jew and participated in Jewish life-cycle rites.

In Orthodox Judaism, the marriage of a Jew to a non-Jew is not recognized. However, conversion is not for the purpose of marriage; a person does not convert with the intent to marry an Orthodox Jew. "It is an ideological state," according to Rabbi Gedalia Dov Schwartz.

The procedure of converting to Judaism is defined in Talmudic Law, the Codes of Jewish Law. The convert renounces all previous affiliation and accepts without exception all the laws of the Torah (the first five books of the Old Testament). "You must acknowledge that, as a Jew, you are in for harassment, persecution, and even violence," Rabbi Schwartz says. "Make up your mind to accept this development and responsibility."

In Orthodox Judaism, each Rabbinical Court has its own standards for conversion. A man must be circumcised and then must perform the rite of immersion in the ritual pool, or mikvah, observed by the three rabbis of the Rabbinical Court. A woman is also immersed in the ritual pool.

In Conservative Judaism, when there is an interfaith relationship, there is a "push for conversion, preferably before marriage," according to Rabbi Vernon Kurtz. "Conversion is a process. It involves education, ritual behavior, and acceptance of a faith system and a peoplehood."

Candidates for conversion attend classes where they study Hebrew and learn about Jewish festivals, the observance of *Shabbat* and kashruth. "Converts are leaving their former religion and accepting Judaism," Rabbi Kurtz says.

In Conservative Judaism, the traditional conversion ritual is followed. Males must be circumcised. If a man is already circumcised, he goes through the symbolic ritual of drawing blood. Both men and women must be immersed in the mikvah. The actual ceremony of conversion is usually private, with the family gathered before the open Ark in the synagogue.

In Reform Judaism, the most liberal of the Jewish sects, conversion is never pushed on the non-Jewish partner. Although the support group, Outreach, does encourage mixed couples to raise their children in a Jewish home, conversion is not a goal.

"With our rabbi, it's almost painfully in the opposite direction," Tom says. "The last thing in the world he would want to be accused of is even suggesting that conversion is the appropriate outcome of Outreach."

In a 1973 resolution declaring its opposition to mixed marriage, the Central Conference of American Rabbis of Reform Judaism called upon its members to "provide the opportunity for conversion of the non-Jewish spouse."

Conversion through the Reform Movement of Judaism has its basic components, according to Rabbi Stephen Hart. The details of how these components are carried out and the time it takes to complete the process differ from rabbi to rabbi and from individual to individual.

The first component is study. The time required to complete the study varies. Rabbi Hart usually requires a fifteen-week Introduction to Judaism, but this requirement is highly individual. Some prospective converts may require two years or more before they are ready for conversion. Others who have already been living a Jewish life-style may not require so long.

The next component is the living or experiential component. Candidates for conversion participate in Jewish experiences; for example, attending *Shabbat* services, bar or bat mitzvah services, and holiday celebrations such as Purim or Sukkoth in the synagogue, as well as attending a *Shabbat* meal and a Passover seder in the home.

The ritual, or ceremonial, component varies the most among rabbis. Some Reform rabbis ask the convert to go to the mikvah for immersion. Others do not require this. Some rabbis ask the male convert to be circumcised; some do not. If a man has been circumcised, a symbolic drop of blood is drawn.

The final step in a Reform Jewish conversion is the ceremony in the synagogue. This may be public, performed at a regular service of the congregation, or it may be a private ceremony, depending on the decision of the rabbi. The candidate for conversion stands in front of the open Ark, says the traditional prayers, literally embraces the Torah, and then receives a Hebrew name. "These are wonderful, wonderful moments," says Rabbi Hart.

When a Muslim woman marries a non-Muslim, the man is required to convert to Islam for the marriage to be recognized. On the other hand, when a non-Muslim woman marries a Muslim, conversion of the woman is not required. Yosef tells about a friend of his family, a Catholic woman who was married to a Muslim for twenty years before she chose to convert.

According to Amir Ali of the Institute of Islamic Information and Education, conversion in Islam is called "accepting." In the ceremony, called Shahadah or "witnessing," the convert declares that the decision is voluntary and not coerced. He pronounces the creed and announces that he is accepting Islam. Circumcision is required of all male converts.

"In Buddhism, rather than a formal ceremony, conversion is mostly a matter of one's own faith," Helen says. "A person embraces the religion and raises the children in the Buddhist way."

Michelle, also a Buddhist, says, "There really was no process for my husband Gary to convert from Christianity to Buddhism. Buddhism and Eastern thinking were not contrary to his thinking, and he readily accepted it."

To convert or not to convert is a personal decision. "You don't do this for your spouse; you do it for yourself, your own faith," says Father Michael Place.

Eileen agrees. "I decided I had to convert for myself, not for Mark or his parents or anybody else."

Cheryl says, "I never asked Patrick to convert, because

that's a very personal thing. It was entirely his choice. In fact, I was very surprised when he told me he had decided to do this."

"I never said, if you marry me you have to believe what I believe," Debbie says. "And I don't want to believe what Mitch believes. Conversion was never an issue with us."

CHAPTER 9

Changes and Choices: Interfaith Teens

C laire Miller and her daughter, Stephie, stood by the front door. They were both dressed in their "Sunday best" clothes. "Michael," Mrs. Miller called, "are you ready to leave? Church services start in twenty minutes."

Fifteen-year-old Michael appeared at his bedroom door. He was wearing the same sweat shirt and torn jeans he had worn to play basketball the day before. "I'm not going to church any more," Michael said. "Religion doesn't mean anything to me."

Mrs. Miller stared at her son in disbelief. Although Michael was being brought up in an interfaith family—his father was Jewish and his mother was Protestant—he had attended Sunday school from a very young age and had participated in many activities at the Protestant church, including the youth group. "I don't understand this sudden change in attitude," Mrs. Miller said. "But I don't have time to discuss it with you now." She took the hand of Michael's sister and left for church.

Michael's attitude may have surprised his mother, but such changes take place frequently. As children grow into adolescents, they want to be more independent and develop their own ideas in many different areas of their lives. Religion is one of those areas subject to change, whether a teenager is growing up in an interfaith family, or with parents who have the same faith. Their choices are influenced by their parents' depth of religious commitment, by their friends' ideas, and by their own personalities.

"Once teenagers are confirmed, they tend to drop out of church life," says Protestant minister Donna Gray. "They have doubts; they want to experiment. Teens are breaking away from their parents, which means they are breaking away from their parents' faith, too. Some take religion class in college, which gives them new insights. They may not come back to the church until they get married, or even until their first child is born."

Some teenagers may strengthen their commitment to religion, whereas others feel less of a commitment or lose interest altogether. Some may even change their religious affiliation. Some young adults do not reject their religion itself, but the objectives of that religion. Many become more interested in social service activities, such as helping the poor, than in observance of religious ritual.

Margo and her father illustrate the contrast in the direction a young adult may take. Margo's father, Ed, was raised a Catholic, but when he went to college, he stopped practicing Catholicism. Ed married a Jewish woman and raised his children in a Jewish home. "My father is almost an assimilated Jew," Margo says. "He is involved in Jewish religious events. He participated in my bat mitzvah and held the Torah."

In contrast, when Margo went to college, she realized the importance of maintaining her Jewish identity. "I know that when some kids get to college, they want to ignore their religious identity," she says. "But I wanted to learn more about my Jewish heritage, the culture and the history, and even the Jewish holidays and prayers. I am planning to go to Israel to live on a kibbutz and learn more there."

As Nick was growing up, he and his parents were actively involved with the Catholic Church. "But when I became a teenager, the church became a pain," Nick recalls. "There were too many rules, too many ways to mess up. It became hard to comply. So when I was old enough, I just chose not to comply."

On the other hand, Nick's wife, Karen, became more active in Jewish religious activities as a teenager. "I belonged to the Jewish Community Center when I was in high school, and Hillel in college," Karen says. "It was more of a social activity than religious."

When Josh became a teenager, he examined his Jewish religion more closely and found much of it unacceptable to him. "When I started thinking about it, I saw general problems such as a girl who got a gold watch because she learned her bat mitzvah three weeks early. It seemed to me that that wasn't what religion is about," Josh says. "It's interesting to me how binding religion can be to some people, and how it's just not important to others."

Eighteen-year-old Stacey also noticed the differences of commitment among her friends. "The year I was in seventh grade, my Sunday school class went from twenty-five people to five people," says Stacey, who was brought up Jewish in an interfaith home. "So many of the kids had their bar and bat mitzvah and then quit. To me, just because you learn a little Hebrew and have a bar mitzvah, I don't think you should quit. If you really believe in this, if you're really into it, you should continue and be confirmed. I thought the whole thing was kind of dumb, to go and learn a language and just pretend."

For Stacey, a college religion course helped strengthen her commitment to Judaism. "My thinking is stronger because I am older," she says. "There is a lot from the Old Testament that I had read when I was younger but did not understand as well as I do now. I had a teacher standing in front of me saying this is what it means, but when you're young, a lot goes in one ear and out the other. Now that I'm older, I'm actually reading it for myself and having to interpret it for myself, and writing papers on it myself. Every week in religion class I had to decide what I really felt. I had to interpret things and see how they added together. I just started feeling stronger about how I fit in. That's when I started thinking that I was Jewish, and not both religions."

Nineteen-year-old Matt, whose mother is Catholic and father is Jewish, was raised a Catholic. He still describes himself as a devout Catholic. Yet, as Matt grew into adolescence, he began to take a serious look at his father's faith. "A ten-year-old rarely examines his religion to a great extent," Matt wrote in a college essay. "It was not until I was seventeen years old that I discovered I had very little knowledge of the Jewish faith. As I reached my later years of adolescence, I began to think seriously about my father's faith and about my own faith. I wondered if it was my obligation to observe and know the significance of Jewish holidays."

*   *   *

As children become adolescents, they begin to formulate their own ideas and religious philosophies. Teenagers are not only formulating ideas about religious affiliation, but also religious identity. That is especially true of interfaith teens. They may not always agree with their parents, even when they have a strong background in a single religion. Although Matt was brought up a Catholic, he does not totally agree with his mother's Catholic philosophy. "I wouldn't agree with some of the particular issues my mother believes," he says. "Opinions vary from family member to family member. I would limit my definition of a Catholic family to belief in Jesus Christ solely."

Matt's brother Howard agrees. "Leave out the more political issues like abortion and such," he says. "Those are not so much differences in religious belief, but different attitudes. It's happening not just in our family, but in most Catholic families."

Another brother, twenty-one-year old Gene, has completely separated himself from the family religion. Although he was raised Catholic, Gene says, "I'm not Catholic. I don't go to church, and I don't have anything to do with the Catholic Church."

Many young adults growing up in interfaith families have no doubts about their religious identity. Howard never questioned his religious identity. "Because I was raised a Catholic, it never came into my mind to ask, Am I a Catholic? Am I a Jew? Instead it was a question of, Am I a Catholic? versus Am I not a Catholic? If this had been a very liberal marriage, and I had been baptized as well as had a bar mitzvah and had all these things going concurrently, I would probably question what I am. I would not have been sure: am I one or the other, am I both? But that never came up."

Although eighteen-year-old Stacey identifies herself as

Jewish, she appreciates both her Christian and Jewish traditions. "I was raised in a family that has background on both sides," Stacey says. "I just happen to be stronger one way."

The religion class Stacey took in college made her think more about her religious identity. "Maybe I signed up for the class in college because I was confused inside," she says. "The class divided up Christianity and Judaism and then tried to put them together. It tried to show how the two religions blended together. It really made you think of what you actually believed in, especially if you are in a position like mine, with some background of both religions."

Stacey's sixteen-year-old brother Brent prefers to identify with the religious traditions of both parents. "We evolved our own religion, sort of a combined thing," Brent says. "As you go on, you take things from both religions and make it into a different type of belief. You take views from both religions and put them into one that you can believe in. I think I'm both, and I've developed my own thoughts."

Margo was always sure of her religious identity. "I am not confused about my identity," she says. "I am not half and half; I am one hundred percent Jewish. I think the only drawback to growing up in an interfaith family is that I am not being educated by both parents. It's more of a cultural or a social problem than a religious problem, but there is something missing. Other Jewish kids can talk to their fathers about Jewish things, and I can't."

Some teens think that being identified as of both religions can be confusing and unsatisfying. Cheryl, the mother of an interfaith family who also grew up in an interfaith family, recalls her own feelings as a teen. "I remember when I was a kid growing up, there were two things that I was struck with," she says. "People would say to me, 'You're half and half, half Jewish and half non-Jewish.' I always resented that, because I was very much a whole person. I wasn't half anything. That always bothered me. The other feeling was that I never quite belonged. I felt that I was never good enough to be part of the Jewish community, and I felt very definitely that I didn't belong in the Christian community."

Sandy, who, like Cheryl, grew up in an interfaith family and is now the mother of one, felt a lot of confusion as a teenager. "As I was growing up, I was always aware that everyone on both sides of the family thought that their religion was the right one," Sandy says. "I worked that out as a teenager, and kind of rejected it all. Even though I was brought up a Catholic, by the time I was an adolescent, I identified much more with my Jewish father than my Catholic mother. I decided I wasn't Catholic anymore, and I said I was going to be Jewish. But it was very naive, because my father didn't really practice Judaism. I thought things would happen magically, but I didn't understand it until I was older. Because we lived in a small town where there were not many Jews, it wasn't until I married someone Jewish that I realized Judaism is very different from what I had thought."

According to social worker Tema Rosenblum, Sandy's situation is not unusual. "When adolescents choose a religion, girls most often choose the father's religion, and boys most often choose the mother's religion."

Some teenagers, like Josh, avoid confusion and choice by not identifying with any religion. "I don't think of myself with any religion," Josh says. "And I don't think I can because I don't go through all the motions and all the beliefs in any particular religion, although there are parts of some beliefs and cultures that I think are quite interesting. What I find especially interesting are stories that teach a point. I have no problem believing those. But I do have problems repeating prayers. That does not ring true to me. I have a bunch of friends who are in the same bind or even more so. They are going through the motions of religion but have come to a point where they don't really believe in it."

Interfaith teenagers may actually be more sensitive about their ethnicity than their religious identity. One nineteen-year-old boy, whose mother is Japanese and whose father is Jewish Caucasian, is shy about being Japanese but he is not shy about being Jewish. He is president of a Jewish fraternity in college. Michelle reports that her daughter Amy is "probably more embarrassed about her Japanese ethnicity than her Buddhist religion."

Teenagers and their parents point out that life in modern society can interfere with religious practice. "The American way of life got in the way," Karen says. "We can't go to the synagogue on Friday nights because Zachary has Boy Scouts. Nick works Sundays, and that puts a crimp in our style, our religious style."

Vera, the mother of two teenagers being brought up Jewish, agrees. "We are caught in the assimilation," she says. "We have to make choices. There are school activities on Shabbat, the Jewish sabbath. When I was growing up as a Protestant, there was no problem. But now our Jewish family is in the minority, and we have to think differently."

"Sometimes our own views do not seem as important as those of the community, " Vera continues. "Many of our teenagers' friends are not Jewish. Parents sometimes feel like they are in competition."

Community attitudes are important. A teenager's religious identity, and how comfortable he or she feels with that identity, may have a lot to do with where the teenager is living and what the social environment is. "I didn't really think much about religion when I was younger, until we moved here," Josh says. "Around here, religion is a little more important to people in general, especially if you are Jewish. Once, I was baby-sitting for a Jewish family. The little boy asked me, 'Are you Jewish?' when he met me. It was almost the first question he asked. It was kind of a surprise, because I didn't think someone's religion was that important. But it is around here."

"My opinions changed when I went to college," Stacey says. "I grew up in an area where there is a good mix of religions, including Jews; but at school there's not. I'm now in the minority. A lot of people had never met a Jewish person before. They wonder about it. They are curious and ask questions. One of my college roommates knew only two Jews her entire life. She came back from spring break and said, 'Guess what, my mom went to a bat mitzvah this weekend.' When I was growing up I went to five every weekend, but she was so excited to tell me that her mom went to one and got to see the whole ceremony. It was weird to see her so excited about something that seemed so normal to me."

Brent says, "When you're a kid, you don't notice everything around you; you just have fun. But as you get older, you realize that some of your friends aren't the same as you. I go to camp for eight weeks. A majority of the kids there are Jewish. I could see that if I wasn't Jewish, it would be kind of hard; it's hard for people who aren't Jewish. As you grow up, you just start realizing how conscious people are of religious differences."

Stacey and Brent's mother, Debbie, notes that there was more discrimination when she was a teenager. "When I went to high school, I really saw the prejudice," Debbie says. "The Catholic boys weren't allowed to date the Jewish girls. When they'd bring me home to their parents, they always gave me a last name that didn't sound Jewish."

Religious differences are less important in an environment with a mixture of faiths. In that situation, teenagers have fewer problems with their interfaith status. They experience less discrimination. Thirteen-year-old Annie has friends of many different religions and heritages. "No matter what religion you are, there is the same relationship," she says. "I don't discriminate, and no one discriminates against me. There is no difference."

Margo believes that growing up in an interfaith family helps a teenager keep an open mind about people of other faiths. "In the homes of my friends where both parents are of the same religion, they seem much more concerned about someone's religion, whether it's a friend or a famous person on television. But I think, who cares? It's who they are first, not what religion they are that's important to me."

People may not even realize they have prejudices. "My two roommates—one is nineteen, and one's eighteen—have known only two Jewish people their whole lives," Stacey says. "Their jokes weren't directed at Jews, but there were little phrases or sayings that are associated with Jewish people. They think that I'm offended, but I'm just laughing because I realize that they don't understand much about it. They do want to learn, because they're curious."

Speaking about her family, Roslyn says, "Lisa and her brothers will not tolerate any derogatory racial comments or religious jokes among their friends or people they come in contact with."

"I have a lot of problems with people accepting me, not so much because of religion, but more because my mom is American and my father is Indian. It's more because it's an interracial marriage than an interreligious family," Roslyn's daughter Lisa says. "As for what religion I was, they did not accept Hinjew as an answer. Even a teacher asked me what my religion was. In junior high school, most of my friends were also children of immigrants. They tended to be more open-minded. I became very selective about my friends in high school.

"I didn't choose my friends because of what religion they were; but I found that, especially when I was dating, the guys chose me because of what I was. No parents ever liked me when I dated their son; they liked me *until* I started dating their son. I don't know why there was such a problem. When you're sixteen, you're not going to marry the guy; you're just going to a dance. Friendship should not be limited by religious or cultural differences, because it is so personal. It shouldn't be a problem, but sometimes it is."

Lisa and Phyllis had been neighbors and friends throughout high school. One day when the two were baby-sitting for another neighbor, they were laughing about their own future families. "Maybe we'll have our babies at the same time and live in the same neighborhood," Phyllis said.

"That would be great," Lisa responded. "And wouldn't it be nice if your daughter and my son got together or visa versa?"

Suddenly, Phyllis looked very serious. "Oh, I wouldn't

allow that. Your children won't be Jewish, so our children won't date."

Lisa was surprised by Phyllis's answer. Earlier in high school, Phyllis had dated a guy who wasn't Jewish, and her mom had been very upset about it. At the time, Phyllis had said, "I'll never do this. I'll never accept my mom's thinking on this."

But now she's the same way, Lisa thought. She's turned out exactly like her mom. She said no to me because I am of a different religion.

There are teens who date only someone of the same religion, as well as many teens who purposely do not date—or do not choose to date—someone of the same religion. Many young people live in an environment that provides a greater opportunity to meet others of different religions and cultures. In today's world of mobility and assimilation, teenagers—whether from interfaith or same-faith homes—are more apt to choose friends and dates who are of different religions. "Although I didn't seek out non-Jewish guys when I was in high school and college, I never felt it would be wrong to date or marry someone who wasn't Jewish," says Sarah, who was brought up Jewish.

On the other hand, Margo grew up in a less diversified area. "I grew up surrounded by Jewish people," she says. "There was not as much opportunity to date non-Jewish guys."

A teenager's religion itself may dictate the type of social life he or she has. Even if their mothers are non-Muslim, Muslim teens do not date or attend mixed parties. In many families, marriages are still arranged by the parents.

Because of their concern about the increase in inter-marriage, many Jewish congregations are also concerned about interdating. They are working with teenagers by sponsoring programs that provide students and their parents an opportunity to talk about interdating and intermarriage. According to Rabbi Stephen Hart, "There is a resources guide put out by the support group Outreach on how to talk about this whole area of adolescence."

"When they are dating, teenagers should ask themselves how religion figures into their relationship," says David Kovacs, who coordinates a support group for Catholic-Jewish families.

Egan Mayer cites a 1983 study showing that children from interfaith families as well as those from families where one parent had converted to Judaism had similar friendship patterns. Most had both Jewish and non-Jewish friends. Most of them felt equally comfortable with both Jews and non-Jews. As teenagers, they dated both Jews and non-Jews, and most said they would not discourage their own children from marrying non-Jews.

Brent says, "When it comes to friends and dating, I think being from an interfaith family is an advantage. You can like anyone you want to. If I have a Jewish girlfriend, I can say I'm Jewish, and everything is fine. And, if I was going out with someone who isn't Jewish, I could just say I wasn't Jewish, and everything would be fine. When you're interfaith, you understand all your friends. You understand your Jewish friends and how they take a lot of stuff for being Jewish. You understand your Christian friends, because you're from both religions. You feel all your friends can talk to you about it. There's no problem. I don't feel that people are prejudiced; no one cracks jokes, anyway."

"I don't think my being from an interfaith family is an influence at all on dating," Stacey says. "I've considered myself more Jewish from the start. My parents never said, you have to marry someone of your faith. It was no big deal. A lot of the guys I've dated have not been like that either. Actually, with a lot of people, religion never even comes up. I'm sure if I was on the verge of getting married, religion would come up and be an issue. But right now, personally I don't have any views. I'm not saying, 'Oh, I have to marry a Jewish person.' It's not that I don't care, but it's not a priority. I am not out looking for that special Jewish person, I'm just looking for that special person, period."

Stacey's mother, Debbie, was brought up in a Jewish home. "My parents never said I couldn't date a guy who wasn't Jewish. Of all my friends who were told they could only date Jewish guys and that they couldn't bring home a guy who wasn't Jewish, every single one of them ended up marrying someone who wasn't Jewish. They were always told, you can't touch, you can't go out with these guys. So when my friends went away to college, they all found guys who weren't Jewish, and they all ended up marrying them. What you couldn't have looked better that what you were used to."

"I think that because we didn't go to a Catholic school, our friends are more diverse," Howard says. "I'm currently dating someone who is Protestant, which is less of a difference than if I were dating someone who was Jewish or some other faith. With me, the same questions have come up, What if we get married? How are we going to raise the kids? Is one of us going to convert? It has broadened my mind to the extent that I see it's possible.

"If I had been raised ten years ago or more and had gone to Catholic schools, I would not have had the broadness of experience to help me make that decision. Marrying a non-Catholic might have been out of the question. I might have had a mother or father who said, 'No, you're marrying a Catholic, and that's it.' My upbringing has been a broader experience, which has been very nice and very helpful."

Howard's brother, Matt, agrees. "It's more of an enlightened thing, a more positive way of growing up."

Their mother, Elena, acknowledges the possibility of her sons intermarrying. "In the most perfect world, in the best of all worlds, I would hope that the boys would marry Catholics," she says. "I don't think that's very likely. I've thought about it recently because the boys are getting to the age when they will be getting married. I hope I can follow the example of my sisters-in-law who have had to face interfaith marriages of all their children. Sometimes there have been conversions of the mate; sometimes there hasn't been a conversion. Regardless, Ray's sisters have handled it so wonderfully, I would look to them as an example. I would wish the boys would marry Catholics. I would like my grandchildren to be Catholic; that would be very important to me."

Vera grew up as a Protestant and converted to Judaism after she married a Jewish man. "As a convert who brought up her children Jewish, it's especially hard for me to see my teenagers dating Catholics," she says. "My children don't understand why it's a problem with me. There is more of a chance that my daughter will bring up her children as Jews, because they will be considered Jewish. I will have to talk to my son more about the Jewish identity of his children."

Many of the young people who grow up in an interfaith family go on to have interfaith families of their own. Others are influenced by that same experience to marry someone of the same faith. Jon, whose mother is Jewish and father is Christian, is being brought up Jewish. He says, "When I grow up, I will never choose anyone who isn't Jewish."

Besides dating and marriage, interfaith teens may consider how they would raise their own families religiously. "I would probably raise my kids in the religion of the person I'm married to, but I could still have my own beliefs," Brent says.

Brent's sister, Stacey, does not see her future the same way. "I would probably raise my children Jewish, especially if I'm married to a Jewish man," she says. "If I married a non-Jew, we would have to talk about it, but I would still want to raise my children Jewish.

"Our temple is very, very Reform. I have already decided that I am going to raise my children in a stronger sect than I was raised in, less radical Reform, if not Conservative. I feel strongly about that. I'd like to raise my children as Conservative Jews."

"My children will get their Jain background from their grandparents," Lisa says. "From me, they'll just get a belief in God and the idea that there are all kinds of religions. My children will be exposed to many religions because we will live in an area that's multi-religious. I want to be sure to live in an area that is open-minded."

Josh says, "I think I would raise my own children the way I am being brought up, as a person of the world. I kind of like it this way. It's what I can believe in, based on human conduct. Be yourself and find your place in society. Being taught what effect you're going to have on society is more important to me than learning about a religion and just going to services."

Interfaith teenagers may feel fewer constraints about their personal choice of religion than teens growing up in same-faith families. As one father said, "I am raising my children in one religion. When they grow up, they may accept it or reject it."

Matt says, "Your choice of religion is really a personal

thing. It's the most personal of all things. In our family, it has never been a topic of discussion. We all respect each other's choice. We may not agree with the other's choice, but we respect it as a personal choice."

CHAPTER 10

Aid and Comfort to the Interfaith Family

The lights in the school building of the Reform synagogue were reflected on the new snow. Tom O'Brien and his wife Janie held hands as they walked up the steps. Tom felt nervous, and he guessed that Janie was, too. They had both been very quiet in the car on the way over, which was unusual for them. It was the first time they had attended a meeting of the support group for interfaith couples. Another interfaith couple had asked Janie and Tom to tell the group about their experiences and how they were coping.

As they approached the classroom where the meeting would take place, Tom noticed many people in the hall having refreshments and chatting. There were other young couples like themselves as well as older people the age of their own parents. Slowly, everyone drifted into the brightly lit classroom and sat down.

As couples started speaking and commenting on the topic of the evening, Tom noticed how much in common he and Janie had with them. "Everyone in the group had such a common experience, it was really a wild feeling," Tom says. "For us, it was so attractive. You walk into this room, and everybody is just like you. How can you not want to join the group?"

As the number of interfaith families grows, so does the number of support groups, special programs, books and articles, and other resources designed to help with their special problems.

Rabbi Stephen Hart says, "A support group provides a forum for interfaith couples to discuss and share their greatest concerns." Groups can be helpful all along the spectrum, from couples just deciding to get married, to married couples with children, to the parents of inter-married couples.

Rabbi Hart is a facilitator for Outreach, a support group for interfaith couples sponsored by Reform Judaism. According to Rabbi Hart, Outreach aims to "reach out to interfaith couples to let them know we embrace them and to encourage them to come into the synagogue, to provide programs that allow them to further investigate the issues that they're struggling with, and to meet all their various needs, everything from holiday celebrations to raising the children and concerns with the extended family. We provide a support system for not only the interfaith couple, but also for the Jew By Choice, the person who converts.

"We try to organize it by topic, and focus each time on a different aspect of intermarriage. But usually before the evening is over we cover the whole range of questions and issues that interfaith couples have. The biggest program of the year, the one that draws the most attention and the most people, is the one around Hanukkah and Christmas: the 'December dilemma.'" Programs may be supplemented with materials such as videos and handouts. Books and pamphlets are available. There are training programs and programming guides for facilitators.

Most support groups are started by Jewish organizations and usually aim to encourage interfaith families to maintain a Jewish household and to raise the children Jewish. However, in most support groups—Jewish or not—there is no agenda for conversion.

Because its programs support the interfaith family and do not promote conversion of the non-Jewish partner, Outreach has been criticized by leaders of Conservative Judaism as "an exercise in futility and a waste of resources." Conservative Rabbi Vernon Kurtz set up a task force to promote Jewish marriage and deal with conversion issues. In an effort to bring people into Judaism and not close the door on them, he established a special *keruv* program (*keruv* meaning "to bring closer"). "We wish to draw the non-Jewish spouse closer to Judaism with the hope that he or she will choose to become one of us," Rabbi Kurtz said in a sermon to his congregation.

Occasionally, a Christian organization sponsors an interfaith support group. An example of a successful group for Jewish-Catholic couples was set up in the Catholic Archdiocese of Chicago. The group's newsletter states that its purpose is to "help people who come from these two great religious traditions deal with some of the issues and questions intrinsic to such a relationship."

Keith, who is Jewish, and his wife, Pat, who is Catholic, helped to organize the group. "Everybody here has something in common," Keith says. He humorously refers to the Catholic-Jewish families as "Cashews."

Pre-Cana classes, which are required of any couple

getting married in the Catholic Church, may address interfaith marriage. "It is very possible that an interfaith couple may be the presenting couple at some of the pre-Cana sessions," Frank Hannigan explains. "This makes other interfaith couples feel comfortable."

Catholic Marriage Encounter may also provide support for interfaith couples. "Marriage Encounter is very ecumenical, with a variety of faiths attending," says one of the sponsors. She estimates that seventy-five percent of the couples who attend the weekend are of mixed faiths or non-Catholic.

Protestant churches occasionally sponsor or simply "house" educational or support groups for families. Interfaith families may participate in the activities of these groups. "It is a mission of our church to provide free space to a family support group," Protestant minister Donna Gray says. "But it is an independent group, not a church group. They serve a lot of interfaith families."

The family that is interested in a support group can find out about one through a priest or rabbi. Where a support group does not exist, one can be organized. One church organized a support group for Catholic-Protestant couples because there were a number of such families attending the church. Some groups are set up specifically for parents who are raising their children in two faiths. A group for doctors and nurses involved in interfaith marriages was established at a large health clinic. "If a couple want to start a group, I would encourage them," Keith says. "All you need is a priest or rabbi and a facility that is an ongoing place."

Karen and Nick belong to a Jewish-Catholic group that meets in a Catholic church. Karen is very enthusiastic about it. "Now I can do a commercial," she says. "This Jewish-Catholic group has been tremendous on so many levels. We felt like pioneers. Nothing like this existed; this was the beginning. But when we started out, all we had were the needs of our interfaith families, wondering which way we were going. The group has grown, even though there's no formal membership. We've reached a point where we've all talked about how our families feel about us, where the problem comes in, whether there is a problem before the children or only after the children. We have committees branching off now. One group is working on how to conduct your marriage ceremony. Another committee is working on education, on how do we educate our children, which to me is the most important thing."

Karen and Nick found out about the interfaith group through some friends at a local synagogue. "We discovered that people in this group had already made their decision," Karen says. "They were raising their children Jewish, except for one couple where the mother was raising one child Jewish and the father was raising the other child Catholic. The value of a support group is being around people who have the same problem. We're not alone. There are people having the same problems. Some have had some success, and they share that success."

Eileen, a Christian married to a Jew, agrees with this opinion. "Before joining Outreach I felt really isolated, like I was the only person on earth making these decisions. You think you're the only two people who have this problem, and then you go to Outreach and see everybody is in some stage of the decision-making process. Here you can find out what the options are, and what other people are doing. And it doesn't get so emotional and so personal as when it's just the two of you and your own family.

"When you're in a relationship, you feel like you should be judging each other, so to go to a place that's really safe and nonjudgmental is such a relief. You can take a deep breath—sort of a sigh of relief—that it's okay to think and feel what we feel."

Janie, who is Jewish, and her husband Tom, a Catholic, are active in Outreach. "There are many times when we walk into the synagogue, and I feel so different from everyone else," Janie says. "I know that the minute I start introducing ourselves, the eyebrows are going to go up. But this group gives us a sense of belonging. We're not the only ones who are intermarried."

"In a support group, everyone is looking for a place to discover what they share," Keith says. "One of the best benefits of a support group is that it is a conversation sparker. Couples leave our meetings and talk to each other. There is always open discussion."

"Things are out in the open and we can talk about them," Tom says. "And you have a chance to discuss a problem when you're not already at wit's end, when you're still rational."

Karen appreciates the opportunity for discussion. "Bringing problems out into the open was beneficial," she says. "I've always had the feeling that part of our problem is being afraid of confronting this. We kind of dance around it, trying to do both religions, and trying to be kind to each other's religion. Not to decide is to decide. The support group also provides us with the knowledge and the resources that we need to cope."

Education and information are additional benefits of support groups. Many offer holiday workshops where the history, meaning, and practice of the religious holidays are discussed. The Catholic-Jewish group sponsors a Passover seder at the Catholic church. Once a year Outreach offers a weekend retreat featuring a speaker who is an expert on intermarriage. "The support group is also educational because each partner can learn about the other's religion and their commonality," Keith says.

Outreach has developed a program called Stepping Stones, which provides a two-year tuition-free Jewish education for the young children of interfaith families that are not affiliated with a synagogue. The program is considered successful because two thirds of the families involved after two years have joined a congregation. "The ultimate goal of this program is the creation of Jewish families and children who are raised as Jews," Rabbi Hart explains. "It is not set up to promote conversion." Stepping Stones also includes family programs and a "parent track," which educates the parents along with the children.

"In the Catholic-Jewish support group, we are considering starting a religious school for the children of couples," Keith says.

Support groups also serve a social function. One group holds an annual picnic in a city park. Their families also get together for Thanksgiving, the one holiday all can share.

"Another nice thing about our group is that you get the parents whose children are in interfaith relationships," Eileen says. "I think it's very beneficial not only for couples to see what other people are doing, but also to hear the parents' side and for parents to hear the children's side and to hear from other parents. It helped me appreciate what my parents are going through."

One man compared his support group to an extended family. "When you see other couples accomplish something, you feel some pride."

"I get to see the positive side," Janie says. "I understand Tom and really appreciate all that he's done and all that he's going through."

Many interfaith couples both need and want to join support groups, according to Dru Greenwood, national director of Outreach. "They want to hear; they want to understand. All of them are trying to work things out in a positive way and do the best they can in the situation. They want support now. They want someone to say, 'Yes, you're good people. There is a place for you here.' "

One husband summed up his feelings by saying, "Belonging to a support group not only saved our relationship but helped us grow as people and helped us learn to communicate and accept our differences."

Sometimes, instead of going to a large support group, interfaith couples and their children seek the aid of a social worker or therapist. Some social workers counsel interfaith families individually or in small groups. Clinical Social Worker Felice Friedman says of her work, "It is important that partners clarify who they are. Groups are very helpful prior to marriage. Some couples decide not to get married."

Social worker Tema Rosenblum conducts family life groups in synagogues. Often she presents a Sunday School class program in which students act out dramatic scenes. One scene that features a girl and her boyfriend of different religions acts as a catalyst for discussion of interdating and intermarriage.

Some support groups do not deal with interfaith problems, but rather help families strengthen the religion with which they have decided to identify. Reform and Conservative synagogues offer Introduction to Judaism classes. These classes are usually a prerequisite for conversion, but they may be of interest to interfaith couples as well as Jewish couples who want to learn more about their religion.

The Islamic converts support group is an intercultural organization. They sponsor discussions as well as social events. There are Muslim summer camps and youth groups where children can play with other Muslim children. At the college level, the Muslim Student Association provides support for students of the Islamic faith.

In the Christian-Buddhist family, Gary and Michelle have found that Dharma school workshops help their family develop the Buddhist life-style. Michelle attended three conferences on Buddhism for teachers; Gary attended one. "Before we had children we were involved in various Buddhist groups on the West Coast," Michelle says.

Lisa belonged to the Association of Indians in America, a youth group of Indians representing all the different languages and cultures within India. "That was the most open-minded place I had been to," Lisa says. "That is where I met my Indian friends; they were from all over India. The parents themselves were open-minded."

Although support groups can be helpful in many ways to intermarried couples and interfaith families, the vast majority of interfaith couples do not belong to support groups. Whether or not to participate in a support group is a very personal decision that varies from family to family. Some families see no need for support groups and may not even be aware that they exist.

"There might be a need for a support group if one partner was fervently Jewish, and the other was fervently Catholic, and the two were fervently in love," says twenty-three-year-old Howard, whose mother is Catholic and whose father is Jewish.

Howard's father, Ray, agrees that their family does not need a support group. "There has never been a competing religion in this household," Ray says. "I am not an observant Jew. I go to High Holiday services, and that's all. I don't participate in any religious organization. In a sense, the need for a support group grows out of a family where there is either active or passive competition. For instance, if the children are Catholic, and I go to services every Friday night and give everybody a cold hard stare as I walk out. But it's not like that here. There is no issue; it is resolved."

Lynn says, "We talked about joining a support group. I was interested from time to time, but Richard hasn't been interested. We have more or less worked out the way we are doing things, and it's a way that I'm certainly happy with."

Debbie agrees with Lynn. "We kind of worked it out our own way," she says. "Mitch and I have been married twenty-one years, and there has never been a problem with being an interfaith family."

Occasionally, attending a support group has a negative effect on the interfaith family. "We almost got a divorce after one meeting," Sam jokes. "Everyone does things so differently. Couples deal with their interfaith marriage in their own way. I steered clear of support groups after that. It just brought out the problems that were lurking there."

Another woman said, "When we attend the support group, we sometimes end up with more questions than answers."

Glenn and Melanie receive a lot of information on

support groups. "But it goes right into the trash," Glenn
says. "Groups assume that because we are intermarried,
we have problems. A support group is there to help
couples solve problems, but we don't have problems."

Some couples, such as Marilyn and Larry, consider
attending a support group but do not follow through.
Marilyn says, "I remember hearing about an interfaith
support group that such and such a rabbi was conducting,
a six-week workshop. I thought, 'Gee, that would be
something for us to do.' There were times when we had a
really knotty problem about the children. But we never
did go."

"I am not formally involved in a support group," Sandy
says. "But I think it's a good thing to do, especially when
your kids reach school age. I think that's when being
interfaith can become a problem."

Books and articles can help interfaith families. They may
help with deciding on the religious identity of the family.
Once the religion is decided upon, books and articles can
help the family to develop that religious identity. Trying
to work out their identity, Richard and Lynn turned to a
guide to various denominations.

Robin says, "Reading children's books gives me a different perspective on my religious school students as well
as my own children."

"When we were first married, I got a book on Reform
Judaism," Elena says. "Even though we were going to
raise our children in a Catholic household, I still wanted
to know about Ray's Jewish heritage and have some of the
traditions here, too."

Karen says, "There was a magazine article about an
interfaith couple—the father was Jewish, and the mother

was Catholic—and how they celebrated Hanukkah and Christmas together. That helped me. I always thought it was okay to have the Jewish star on top of the Christmas tree. It was okay for us; it meant something to us. But other people in my family had made comments about how it was wrong. When I read that article, I found out that other people were doing it. They didn't do it carelessly; it had meaning to them. Then I felt better with myself for the decision. That article affirmed that we're not alone. We were not the first ones to think of the idea. It is okay."

It is okay seems to be the reassurance, the aid and comfort, that interfaith couples and families are looking for and finding in books and articles and support groups. As Eileen says, "The group validated my feelings. Now I know there are other people with these feelings. It's okay to have these feelings, and I'm not crazy!"

CHAPTER 11

"It Works for Us"

"We have some interfaith friends; he is from New York and very very Jewish, and she is from San Francisco and Catholic," Sandy says. "They have a wonderful marriage. They've been married a long time. They were always the model of what I was trying to do, although Christine is much more religious than I am. They celebrate everything, and they talk about all of it. Christine is still very observant; she goes to church. The kids go to church, and they go to the synagogue, too. They all go together. They're just exposed to everything, and they talk about everything. It may sound like a recipe for disaster, but it's not. The children are being brought up not in one religion or both at the same time, but they're much more aware of religion. That's the way I wanted things to be."

Every family is special, whether the parents are of the same faith or different faiths. Every family has problems, some more than others. Every family has a different way of dealing with its problems and coping. No matter what activity someone engages in—playing the violin, shooting baskets, or learning French—that person must work at it. It's the same with a family. As teachers and parents often say, "you get out of something what you put into it."

Parents and children describe many benefits from living in an interfaith family: the strengthening of each partner's spirituality, a tendency to be more accepting and open-minded about differences, the opportunity to explore and learn about more than one religion, and the inclination to work harder at communication and compromise.

Bringing two religions together can strengthen the spirituality, the religious feelings, of a family, rather than weaken them. "We now have different insights into two ways of finding God," says Elena, a Catholic married to a Jew.

"Patrick and I have really grown into our Judaism together," Cheryl says. "It has been very unifying for us, as a couple and as a family. The family that we have in a religious sense is very different from those that we grew up with. Patrick is from a religious family; he always had a belief in God. I am from an ethnically Jewish but not religious family. So our family is sort of a combination of the two."

After struggling with their own religious feelings, Renee and Roger were able to resolve differences and strengthen their spirituality. "Now I can feel that our family is experiencing religion together in the broad sense," Renee says. "It's been wonderful for me."

"The irony is that, because I married a non-Jew, I am leading a more active Jewish life, a more active temple life," Janie says. "If I had married a Jew, I might never go near the temple."

Janie's husband, Tom, says, "I'm one of fifteen brothers and sisters, with a very rigid Irish Catholic upbringing.

Probably none of my brothers and sisters regularly goes to church anymore. I'm sure there's a lot more spirituality on my part."

Because they live with differences every day, the parents and children of interfaith families more readily accept differences in other people. "Children have a wonderful capacity to accept differences in a way that adults can't," Cheryl says.

Debbie says, "I think it's nice knowing about a lot of different things, having an open mind, and being able to accept both sides. It doesn't bother me what other people believe, and I don't feel that I'm the only one who is right. If I had been born in Mitch's family, I would have been a Christian. I happen to have been born to Jewish parents, and so I am Jewish."

"In an interfaith family that works, as this one does, there is an openness of mind," Howard, twenty-three, says. "But it's not a laxness, like, 'Wow, I can do anything.' Your vision is clearer with two faiths. There's a wider scope of what you can deal with. You're more adaptable to situations relating to religion and life-styles. It's a learning experience."

"One of the benefits of growing up in an interfaith family is that the children are not being raised in some isolated little corner," Marilyn says. "It's nice for them to be exposed to more than just one faith. They are being given a broader view of things, a realization of differences among people. Just the other day, one of my sons told me, 'When I get married, I'm going to marry someone who's Jewish or Christian or anything I want.' I answered, 'You sure will do exactly what you want.' When I was growing up, I felt I should restrict myself to Jewish men, although I married a non-Jew. My sons can marry anyone they want and feel that it's part of their heritage whether their spouse is Jewish or Christian or even Muslim."

"Children who live in interfaith families are not ghettoized," Patrick says. "They are very comfortable with children of other faiths."

"The best thing that I got from being interfaith was this feeling that there are all kinds of ways to find the truth and to be good in the world. Nobody has the only truth," says Sandy, who was brought up in an interfaith family and is now the mother of one.

Knowing and appreciating other religions enriches a child's life. And living in an interfaith family can provide an opportunity for adults—parents and grandparents as well as the children—to learn about another religion. "I love learning about Judaism and participating in the Jewish holidays," says a Christian woman whose grandchild is being raised Jewish.

While remaining faithful to their own religion, interfaith partners should become acquainted with the beliefs and practices of the other's religion. "When we know about more than one faith, it is a positive thing. We can relate better to our neighbor," says Protestant minister Donna Gray. "Teenagers, especially, should be encouraged to experience different faiths, their own and others. Be with the people of other faiths and even worship with them. Some synagogues and churches provide opportunities for this kind of experience."

An interfaith parent says, "Children in an interfaith family are lucky. They can learn firsthand about two religions."

"I think learning from experience and learning from

those around me is more of a benefit than the religions themselves," says fifteen-year-old Josh.

Eleven-year-old Zachary, who is being brought up Jewish and Catholic, recognizes the advantage of the openness of an interfaith family. "I get to experience more than just one religion. For the time being, while I'm a kid, I'm not stuck in one religion. I can explore the other religions. I get a taste of the major religions. Jewish and Catholic to me are the major religions. If I'm missing anything, I don't know about it."

"My original thought was that living in a Catholic-Protestant family would be a benefit to my children," Claudia says. "I felt that they would have a broader view of their faith by being exposed to both sides of Christianity. I don't feel I know enough about all the different denominations. But I think this way my children will grow up understanding the differences between Catholic and Protestant and be able to choose more intelligently how they want to practice their own faith."

Nineteen-year-old Matt recognizes that there are also some families who are not open-minded. "Some families have a different point of view from us. I see parents who are so fervently religious that they won't allow their children to join organizations or date people of a different faith. Those kids aren't able to learn about other religions."

Often, interfaith couples must work harder than same-faith couples to keep their marriage and their family running smoothly. This can actually be a benefit of living in an interfaith family.

Interfaith couples or families may have the same religion-based problems as other families, but they work harder on them. A rabbi says, "Interfaith couples have more commitment on all issues. They have better communication skills. They communicate on a level common-faith couples never do. They really learn to talk to each other."

"I feel that we could get through absolutely anything now, because of all the time and energy we put into communicating," Eileen says. "We really know each other very well."

Roger says, "To me, one of the benefits of our interfaith family is that it gives me pleasure—and I hope it has given Renee pleasure—knowing that we have taken a very difficult situation and worked through it intellectually. If financial or other difficult problems surface, we can work through them with this as a model. I look at it as a strength now. It was an uphill battle, but now we can fall back on it as a source, a model of what to do in our marriage."

"You are giving your child the gift of compromise. What greater compromise than two faiths in a marriage," said one parent.

Although they acknowledge the special benefits of having an interfaith family, parents admit that there are also special problems: feelings of not belonging, conflicts over religious identity, and questions about celebrating religious holidays. One man put it simply: "It is harder to be intermarried."

Eric, a Catholic married to a Protestant, says, "Intermarriage is a pain in the behind. It's inconvenient and unproductive. Life would be a lot simpler if you went to the same church."

"We have not yet had to explain to the kids why we are doing this. I think that that is going to be a downside,"

Eric's wife Claudia says. "At some point they are going to ask us why we do this. I think it would be nice if we all went to the same church. It would make life simpler; we wouldn't have this sort of competing interest, no matter how muted it may be. There wouldn't be any differences in direction.

"I don't think we've worked it out. From my point of view, this is more difficult that I expected. It's more of an issue than I thought I would make it. I thought it was going to be wonderful for the kids, because they could go for a few years to the Catholic church and a few years to the Protestant church and get a whole nice overview. But I don't know if that's going to work out. I don't know if things are going to turn out the way I envisioned them."

"I didn't acknowledge the differences in our religions as a problem until much later in our marriage," Sandy says. "Early on, when I first converted, I just threw myself into it. Later, when the marriage didn't work out, I realized that we really were two very different people with two very different goals, and that part of that was religion. I'm not saying that it can't work; I'm just saying that it's an issue.

"I've always been aware that religion works two ways. It brings people together, and it also divides people. Growing up with a Catholic and a Jewish parent in the 1950s, I was disowned by one set of relatives because I was Catholic and the other set because I was Jewish. I was never quite a member of any family. I was aware of being the outsider."

Sandy believes that another problem with being interfaith is the issue of identity. "I wish that our family had traditions that felt like they were totally ours," she says. "I miss that kind of connection. Christmas doesn't feel right. Nothing feels right. I don't have a place I can call home religiously. Now I'm sending my children out into the world, and they're going to be in the same bind I'm in, which is both a blessing and a curse. We don't like to say it out loud, but if you're in an area where people need to identify you and determine whether they want to be your friend or not by what religion you are, you're pretty much excluded all around. I don't think it's an accident that the friends we've made are like us, without any strong religious identity."

"One of the most difficult aspects of an interfaith family—no, an interfaith marriage—is the feeling of not belonging to one particular religion," Renee says. "The family fits in, the children fit in, but the couple don't fit in. Sometimes I just feel like an outcast, uncomfortable in some situations. Really, the most difficult part of inter-marriage is feeling that you don't fit in."

Roger agrees. "In an interfaith marriage, someone ends up giving. It's hard for that person to figure out where they fit."

Even if a couple have agreed on the religious identity of their children, each partner wants to maintain his or her own religious identity. A Jewish man married to a Christian woman said, "Before we met the person of another religion, we had twenty or more years of our own religion."

"Interfaith couples have more issues to grapple with," says a rabbi. "Same-faith couples don't talk about identity."

Roger says, "Early in our marriage Renee was very sensitive that, although she was married to a Christian, she wanted to be free to have a Jewish home. She would be doubly difficult about things. I, on the other hand, was fighting for my rights, wanting to participate in my holidays. I think that most of the giving has come from me. In our family, it's four against one."

Even when parents like Roger are willing to raise the children in the religion of the other parent, they may have problems developing their own spiritual feeling for their partner's religion. "It's been very difficult for me to figure out the religion aspect," Roger says. "I feel on the fence. I was born into a Christian family. I was confirmed. I prayed to Jesus Christ. Now I feel that, if I believe in Jesus Christ, it will separate me from my family spiritually, and maybe practically because I'd be so different in their everyday lives. I really can't do that. So I try to understand Judaism. But for a long time it didn't feel spiritual to me."

Roger's wife, Renee, says, "I remember thinking how easy it would be to be sucked into the Christian world. It is so easy for Christians to be Christian. They have no idea how difficult it is to be Jewish. It was important to maintain my heritage."

"I think two-faith marriages would have it a lot easier if the people involved didn't feel as strongly about their faith as Eric and I do," Claudia says.

"What usually happens is that a couple decide on one religion or the other, and they raise the kids as Jews or Catholics or Episcopalians," Eric says. "One of the parents either converts or starts going to a different church. We didn't do that. The differences don't have anything to do with God; they have to with who runs the church, who sets the rules, and what the rules are."

"It's the rules that bother me," Claudia explains. "It bothers me that my children can't have their second communion unless they are baptized in the Catholic Church. Because I'm not Catholic, I'm not supposed to go to the church. I can't take communion as part of the service. Perhaps one of the reasons I wouldn't want to start going there is that I might feel that the Catholic Church wants me to close the door on my whole life's religion and become a Catholic. I couldn't just be a Christian and be part of their church. I think that religion should be a lot more ecumenical than it is in this day and age."

Eighteen-year-old Stacey says, "It is difficult when you tell people that you're both religions. How can they understand? They think it's impossible, because the religious beliefs are so opposite. How can you be looking for the Messiah, as Jews do, and also say the Messiah has already come, as Christians do. How can people understand that? Some beliefs run into each other in life."

Parents may worry about the spiritual feelings of their children in an interfaith home. "The biggest short-term problem is self-doubt," says Karen, "because we have no guidelines. We alternately believe that bringing Zachary up in two religions is the best and the worst thing for him. I don't know if he has feelings of reverence. Intellectually, he can talk about God, he can talk about both religions. But I don't know how much he owns in his heart. Also, Zachary does not participate in the life-cycle events of either religion. He hasn't been baptized, and he won't be bar mitzvahed. That is disappointing to us as well as to his grandparents.

"That's the disadvantage of being diplomatic. We were not sure how to address things, so we backed off a little bit and maybe didn't impress certain things upon Zachary. We wonder, when do you stop impressing upon Zachary the principles of both religions, because at some point they are going to conflict. At that point you make a decision to go one way or another way. But we made the opposite decision—not to send him in a given direction, but to send him in both directions, in a limited way."

Social worker Tema Rosenblum counsels families, some of which are interfaith. "Some interfaith families work out well when one parent is not religious," she says. "They do better. There is more confusion when both parents are devout. Where there is no religion, there is no problem; but parents still wonder if they are doing the right thing."

When there are cultural or ethnic differences as well as religious differences, more problems can occur. Michelle, a Japanese-American Buddhist married to an American Christian, says a difficulty is her lack of understanding of Christian principles and her distance from Western thought patterns. Amir Ali points out, "When a Muslim man marries a non-Muslim woman, he may not tell his wife everything about the culture. These men take advantage of their wives."

Many families cope with interfaith issues by methods that might be used to deal with any family situation: respect, compromise, and communication.

"I think you just have to have respect," Ray says. "It is a matter of mutual respect for what someone else wants to do. It's terribly difficult to ask an adult to change his or her beliefs, whether political or religious. You need to respect an attitude, as long as it's moral. That's everybody's own choice."

Not only the interfaith couple, but the couple's parents need to show respect. Melanie and Glenn came from backgrounds that were different in culture as well as religion. "Both sets of parents as well as we went into the marriage with acceptance and respect for each other's heritage," Melanie says.

"Each partner should respect the other's religion and accommodate it," social worker Rosenblum says. "Support for the other's religion can lead to understanding and being comfortable with the family."

Father Michael Place says, "Have respect for the other's conscience and beliefs. Don't use your faith differences as a scapegoat for personality differences."

"Every marriage has personality clashes," Amir Ali says. "Interfaith marriages have cultural clashes. Problems can be solved by trying to understand the other person's religion and culture. Keep talking; keep an open mind."

Nineteen-year-old Matt repeats those words. "Keep an open mind. Children may be raised in one religion, but while you are raising your children one way, let them know that religion is a matter of personal choice. I would tell children, learn from your parents, keep an open mind."

Claudia agrees. "I don't think that differences are really much more than personal preferences. I think we each accept the other's religion as being a legitimate religion. It's just that there are things about it we don't agree with. We as adults don't necessarily want to change."

It is important to compromise. When conflict occurs, the interfaith couple must settle it between themselves. Their own opinions and feelings are more important than those of their parents or others outside the family. They must make decisions together. "It is the give and take of life," Renee adds. "We have learned to compromise."

Muslim couples, as well as interfaith couples, come to Amir and Mary Ali for counseling. "Most problems are a result of misunderstanding," Amir says. "What is right in one culture may not seem right in another, but it may only be a matter of using the proper language. Think about what the person is saying, appreciate his or position, and express your own position. Often you will find that you are not fighting, you are agreeing."

"When you make decisions, you can come up with some kind of compromise, which is what takes place in any kind of relationship," says Eileen. "You reach a compromise, so next time it will be a little easier."

When compromising on issues, interfaith couples and families may find that they have more in common than not. "Gary and I feel that the differences in our religions and cultures are far less than the similarities," Michelle says. "I find religions more similar than different."

Melanie and Glenn share this philosophy. "Take the best from both traditions. Find the commonality," Glenn says. "Both the Chinese and Jewish heritages honor family, education, survival. They are practical philosophies. As cultures, there is no conflict; their beliefs match."

"Communicate not only your differences, but your common faith," Father Place says. "Although there are definitely differences among faiths, there is much more in common. Build your marriage and your family around those common ideas."

That is also the suggestion of Frank Hannigan. "Look for the commonality, the similarities. Learning about another religion is wonderful. Couples should work together on what brought them together in the first place. Use religion to bring you together, not drive you apart."

Father Ron Scarlatta points out that, although they may be approached in different ways, the moral values of the major religions are similar. Besides a common belief in God, there are prayers and readings that can be shared.

"Both parents have supposedly been raised with the

same general moral background," says twenty-three-year-old Howard. "They both have the Judeo-Christian base. Some of the specific beliefs may be different, but they still come from the same general camp."

Sixteen-year-old Brent agrees. "Even in the same religion, everyone doesn't believe in the same way." Couples should respect the differences, but look for the commonality of their beliefs.

Social worker Felice Friedman says that to cope in an interfaith family, communication as well as compromise is important. "Keep communicating. Don't cover up problems," she says. "Children have questions. Keep communication open to them."

"Talk, talk, talk," is the advice of another social worker. "Problems in an interfaith family are with the religions, not the people."

Communication and compromise are important when making decisions. Melanie and Glenn say that there were three "turning points" in their lives that they consciously discussed and decided: their wedding; whether to have their son Scott circumcised; and starting Annie in religious school.

Many of the interfaith families that cope well minimize the differences. Many say the same thing: "It's no big deal."

"When it comes to issues related to being good people, there is no difference between one religion and another," Eric says. "It is all a question of form over substance. The real benefit of our interfaith family is that the kids understand there's not that much difference. They see Mom and Dad; one's a Catholic, one's a Protestant. We hope they will understand that it's not such a big deal. The differences are kind of unimportant."

"I never thought it was that important," Mitch says, referring to his and Debbie's different religions. "We're all in the same house, but in different rooms. Don't tell me anyone has all the truth. It is more important for you to be a good person, be good to people, be honest, work hard at everything; more than because you're one religion or two religions, or because you're half and half. We didn't make religion the big deal."

Mitch's son, sixteen-year-old Brent, says, "Don't make it a problem. Take advantage of being interfaith rather than thinking of it as a disadvantage. It is an advantage to learn both religions. I have parents who still love each other. It didn't matter to them that they're different religions. They can still have a family, and they can still have everything the same way. It didn't affect anything. A lot of people wouldn't be able to do that; it depends on the parents."

Howard says, "No matter how difficult it may be, keep trying. Keep an open mind. Keep trying to decide for yourself what you want to take as your life stance. Look at others. You've already had the experience; you've seen the Judeo-Christian background. Look at other religions, don't just look at those two."

Fifteen-year-old Josh thinks that young people can cope in an interfaith family by creating a set of personal religious beliefs. "In some ways you have to take in all the information around you, and then you have to completely ignore it and just say, okay, here's what I believe. First you say, here's what my mom believes, and here's what my dad believes, here's what my aunt and my cousins twice removed believe. You take little bits from each and believe in what sounds right to you."

Josh's mother, Sandy, seems to agree with this philosophy. "It's a really good feeling when you're able to
look around and take in all these mixed signals and feel
that you have come up with your own set of beliefs,"
Sandy says. "You may not be able to act it out; you may
not be able to have it all absolutely your own way. But
then in fact it is a personal choice."

Glossary

affiliation Formal association with a religious group or congregation.

assimilation The process of one group's adopting the characteristics of another culture.

baptism Christian sacrament using water symbolically to cleanse recipients of sin and to admit them into Christianity.

bar mitzvah Ceremony recognizing a thirteen-year-old boy as an adult in the Jewish community; *bat mitzvah* or *bas mitzvah* are similar ceremonies for girls.

betsuin Large Buddhist congregation or house of worship.

caste One of four distinctly separate classes into which Hindu society is divided.

catechism Basic instruction or principles of a religion, usually in question and answer form.

Caucasian Of the white race or European descent; not African or Asian.

chrismation Confirmation in the Eastern Orthodox Church; a person is anointed with chrism, or holy oil, sealing the baptism.

christening The Christian sacrament of baptism, including the naming of an infant.

circumcision Religious ceremony in Judaism and Islam in which the foreskin of a male's penis is removed.

clergy People given the authority to perform religious services.

communion Christian sacrament, partaking of bread and wine in celebration of Christ's Last Supper.

confirmation In Christianity, a rite admitting a baptized person to full membership in a church; in Judaism, a ceremony marking the completion of a young person's religious training.

conversion The process of adopting a different religion.

crucifix An image of Christ on the cross.

denomination Group of religious congregations called by the same name; for instance, Presbyterian.

diocese; archdiocese District of churches under a bishop's jurisdiction; a diocese under the juridsiction of an archbishop.

dispensation Exemption from a church law or obligation granted by a church authority.

ecumenical Referring to a movement seeking to achieve unity among religions through cooperation and understanding.

ethnicity Belonging to a particular racial, national, or cultural group; the common characteristics of members of that group.

hajj The pilgrimage of a Muslim to Mecca made during Ramadan.

identity Characteristics by which a person is recognized as a member of a particular group.

karma In Buddhism, the total effect of a person's deeds, determining his destiny.

Koran (Qur'an) The sacred text of Islam, containing the messages from Allah to Muhammad.

kosher Food processed, prepared, and served according to Jewish dietary laws.

Lent Christian observance of fasting and penitence during the forty days from Ash Wednesday to Easter.

mass In the Roman Catholic and some Protestant churches, a religious service including communion.

nonsectarian Not limited to or associated with a particular religious group.

officiate; co-officiate To perform the duties of authority—such as a judge or clergyman—at a wedding ceremony; performing those duties with another member of the clergy.

168 ◇   COPING IN AN INTERFAITH FAMILY

parish In Catholicism and some other Christian denominations, a part of a diocese that has its own church.

Ramadan Ninth month of the Islamic calendar, marked by fasting from sunrise to sunset.

sacrament Formal Christian ritual, such as communion, baptism, or marriage.

Sanskrit Ancient language of India that is the language of Hinduism.

secular Not religious or relating to a religion.

spirituality Sensitivity to religious values.

sutra Statements of principles incorporated in Hindu and Buddhist literature.

Torah Scroll comprising the first five books of the Bible, the basis of all Jewish law and literature.

trinitarian Believing in the Holy Trinity: Father, Son, and Holy Ghost.

unitarian Christian who rejects the doctrine of the Trinity.

Appendix

RESOURCES

Organizations

Listed below are organizations that offer programs of interest to teenagers, either interfaith or same-faith, and to interfaith families. Programs and support groups may often be found at local houses of worship and social service agencies. Where a group or program does not exist, most members of the clergy are willing to help organize one. On college campuses, chaplains of various denominations are available as resources.

Association of Asian Indians in America
300 Clover Street
Rochester, NY 14610
(716) 288-3874
   Twelve state groups that seek "to continue Indian cultural activities in the U.S."

B'nai B'rith Hillel Foundations
1640 Rhode Island Avenue NW
Washington, DC 20036
(202) 857-6560
   Groups on college campuses that provide "cultural, social, educational, religious, social action, and counseling services to Jewish college students," including programs of open discussion on interfaith families and interdating.

B'nai B'rith Youth Organization
1640 Rhode Island Avenue NW
Washington, DC 20036
(202) 857-6633
  Local groups for high school and junior high school students.

Common Ground
815 Rosemary Terrace
Deerfield, IL 60015
(708) 940-7870
  Classes and discussion groups for high school and college
  students on religious and interfaith themes; audio tapes and
  bulletins are available.

Family and Community Services
Many of these agencies offer educational programs, including
programs for families and teenagers, and counseling for families
and interfaith families.

  Family Services of Los Angeles
  1521 Wilshire Boulevard
  Los Angeles, CA 90048
  (213) 484-2944

  Human Services
  838 Grant Street
  Denver, CO 80203
  (303) 830-2714

  Family and Child Services of Washington
  929 L Street NW
  Washington, DC 20001
  (202) 289-1510

  Jewish Family Services of Greater Miami
  1790 SW 27th Street
  Miami, FL 33145
  (305) 445-0555

Jewish Family Services
1605 Peachtree Road, NE
Atlanta, GA 30309
(404) 873-2277

Jewish Family Services
5750 Park Heights Avenue
Baltimore, MD 21215
(301) 466-9200

Family Services of Greater Boston
34 1/2 Beacon Street
Boston, MA 02108
(617) 523-6400

Jewish Family Services (Detroit)
24123 Greenfield Road
Southfield, MI 48075
(313) 559-1500

Jewish Family and Children's Services
9385 Olive Boulevard
St. Louis, MO 63132
(314) 993-1000

Jewish Board of Family and Children's Services
120 West 57th Street
New York, NY 10019
(212) 582-9100

Jewish Family Service Association of Cleveland
2060 South Taylor Road
Cleveland, Ohio 44118
(216) 371-2600

Jewish Family and Children's Agency of Philadelphia
1610 Spruce Street
Philadelphia, PA 19103
(215) 545-3290

Family Guidance Center
2200 Main Street
Dallas, TX 75201
(214) 747-8331.

Islamic Society of North America
P.O. Box 38
Plainfield, IN 46168
(317) 839-8157
Sponsors Muslim Students Association of the U.S. and
Canada, and Muslim Youth of North America.

Pareveh, the Alliance for Adult Children of Jewish-Gentile
Intermarriage
3628 Windom Place, NW
Washington, DC 20008
(202) 363-7266
"We answer questions of all kinds for anyone whose life is
touched by intermarriage," says director Leslie Goodman-
Malamuth. The organization publishes a newsletter and
offers audio tapes of interest to interfaith teenagers.

Rabbinic Center for Research and Counseling
Rabbi Irwin H. Fishbein
128 East Dudley Avenue
Westfield, NJ 07090
(908) 233-0419
Provides a list of rabbis who officiate at intermarriages.

Reform Jewish Outreach

Local groups offer programs for intermarried couples and
couples contemplating intermarriage, as well as the children
of intermarried couples; also programs for Jewish youth on
interdating, intermarriage, and Jewish identity.

Union of American Hebrew Congregations
Central Conference of American Rabbis
838 Fifth Avenue
New York, 10021
(212) 249-0100

Canadian Council
1520 Steeles Avenue West
Concord, Ontario
Canada L4K 2P7
(416) 660-4666

Great Lakes Council
100 Wost Monroe Street
Chicago, IL 60603
(312) 782-1477

Mid-Atlantic Council
61 G Street SW
Washington, DC 20024
(202) 488-7429

Midwest Council
10425 Old Olive Street Road
St. Louis, MO 63141
(314) 997-7566

New Jersey/West Hudson Valley Council
1 Kalisa Way
Paramus, NJ 07652
(201) 599-0080

Northeast Council
1330 Beacon Street
Brookline, MA 02146
(617) 277-1655

Northeast Lakes Council/Detroit Federation
25550 Chagrin Boulevard
Beachwood, OH 44122
(216) 831-6722

Northern California Council
Pacific Northwest Council
703 Market Street
San Francisco, CA 94103
(415) 392-7080

Pacific Southwest Council
6300 Wilshire Boulevard
Los Angeles, CA 90048
(213) 653-9962

Pennsylvania Council
2111 Architects Building
117 South 17th Street
Philadelphia, PA 19103

Southeast Council/South Florida Federation
Doral Executive Office Park
3785 NW 82nd Avenue
Miami, FL 33166
(305) 592-4792

Southwest Council
12700 Hillcrest Road
Dallas, TX 75230
(214) 960-6641

Young Buddhists Association
1710 Octavia Street
San Francisco, CA 94109
(415) 776-5600

Newsletters

Dovetail
Dovetail Publishing
3014A Folsom Street

Boulder, CO 80304
(303) 444-8713
A newsletter "by and for Jewish-Christian families."

Jewish Ties
1091 Quaker Road
Barker, NY 14012
(716) 795-3709
An "independent newsletter for interfaith couples, Jews by choice, Jews by birth, and their families."

For Further Reading

NONFICTION

Brown, Stephen F. *Christianity.* (World Religions Series.) New York: Facts on File, 1991.

Cowan, Paul and Rachel. *Mixed Blessings: Marriage Between Jews and Christians.* New York: Doubleday, 1987.

Edwards, Gabrielle I. *Coping with Discriminations.* New York: The Rosen Publishing Group, Inc., 1986.

Einstein, Stephen J., and Kukoff, Lydia. *Every Person's Guide to Judaism.* New York: UAHC Press, 1989.

Eliade, Mircea, and Couliano, Ivan P. *The Eliade Guide to World Religions.* San Francisco: Harper San Francisco, 1991.

Gay, Kathlyn. *Changing Families: Meeting Today's Challenges.* Hillside, NJ: Enslow Publishers, Inc., 1988.

Goodman-Malamuth, Leslie, and Margolis, Robin. *Between Two Worlds: Choices for Grown Children of Jewish-Christian Parents.* New York: Pocket Books, 1992.

Gordon, Matthew S. *Islam.* (World Religions Series.) New York: Facts on File, 1991.

Kukoff, Lydia. *Choosing Judaism.* New York: Union of American Hebrew Congregations, 1981.

Morrison, Martha, and Brown, Stephen F. *Judaism.* (World Religions Series.) New York: Facts on File, 1991.

Paulson, Terry L. and Sean D. *Secrets of Life Every Teen Needs to Know.* San Juan Capistrano: Joy Publishing, 1990.

Petsonk, Judy, and Remsen, Jim. *The Intermarriage Handbook: A Guide for Jews and Christians*. New York: Quill, 1988.

Reuben, Steven Carr. *A Guide to Interfaith Marriage: But How Will You Raise the Children?* New York: Pocket Books, 1987.

Rice, Edward. *The Five Great Religions*. New York: Four Winds Press, 1973.

———. *Ten Religions of the East*. New York: Four Winds Press, 1978.

Ross, Nancy Wilson. *Buddhism: A Way of Life and Thought*. New York: Alfred A. Knopf, 1980.

Speight, R. Marston. *God Is One: The Way of Islam*. New York: Friendship Press, 1989.

Tames, Richard. *Islam*. (Dictionaries of World Religions Series.) London: Batsford Academic and Educational, 1985.

Wangu, Madhu Bazaz. *Hinduism*. (World Religions Series.) New York: Facts on File, 1991.

Wood, Angela. *Judaism*. (Dictionaries of World Religions Series.) London: Batsford Academic and Educational, 1984.

FICTION

Blair, Cynthia. *Crazy in Love*. New York: Ballantine, 1988.

Brown, Fern. *Our Love*. New York: Fawcett Juniper, 1986.

Cannon, A.E. *The Shadow Brothers*. New York: Delacorte Press, 1990.

Cohen, Barbara. *People Like Us*. New York: Bantam, 1987.

Hamilton, Virginia. *Arilla Sun Down*. New York: Greenwillow Books, 1976.

Hotze, Sollace. *A Circle Unbroken*. New York: Clarion Books, 1988.

Irwin, Hadley. *Kim/Kimi*. New York: Macmillan, 1987.

Kerr, M.E. *Him She Loves?* New York: Harper and Row, 1984.

———. *What I Really Think of You.* New York: Harper and Row, 1982.

Lasky, Kathryn. *Pageant.* New York: Four Winds Press, 1986.

Levy, Marilyn. *Love Is Not Enough.* New York: Fawcett Juniper, 1989.

Marzollo, Jean. *Do You Love Me, Harvey Burns?* New York: Dial Books for Young Readers, 1983.

Meyer, Carolyn. *Denny's Tapes.* New York: Margaret K. McElderry Books, 1987.

Miklowitz, Gloria D. *The War Between the Classes.* New York: Delacorte Press, 1985.

Potok, Chaim. *Davita's Harp.* New York: Alfred A. Knopf, 1985.

Pullman, Philip. *The Broken Bridge.* New York: Alfred A. Knopf, 1992.

Viglucci, Pat Costa. *Cassandra Robbins, Esq.* Madison, WI: Square One Publishers, Inc., 1987.

Index

A

Ali, Amir, 36, 40, 119, 160, 161

B

baptism, 35, 48, 53, 54, 90–91,
   158
   adult, 35, 93, 115
   ecumenical, 55, 91–92
bar/bat mitzvah, 15, 35, 91, 93,
   99, 103, 118, 123
Bronstein, Rabbi Herbert, 11,
   27, 54
Buddhism, 11, 18, 35, 40–41,
   43–44

C

Catholic Conference, United
   States, 3, 12
Catholicism, 14, 35, 37–38, 60,
   70
Central Conference of American
   Rabbis, 10, 118
children
   religious education of, 5–7,
     11, 29–31
   religious identity of, 45–62
chrismation, 35
Christian Orthodox, 3–4, 23,
   29, 35, 38, 53, 66, 85
Christmas, 36, 38, 42, 65, 69,
   75–77, 78, 79, 80, 101, 140
   tree, 17, 49, 58, 75–77, 78,
     79, 80, 81, 83–84
circumcision, 34, 117, 118, 119,
   163
communication, 41, 160
   intrafamily, 151, 154–155,
     162
   with parents, 24–25
communion, 158
   first, 35, 39, 92–93, 95, 99
   inter-, 55
   open, 39
community, religious attitude
   of, 72–74
compromise, intrafamily, 85–
   86, 151, 155, 160–163
confirmation, 35, 91, 93, 99,
   115, 116
conversion, 64, 97, 107–120
   to Buddhism, 119
   to Catholicism, 12, 108, 113–
     115
   to Christian Orthodox, 115
   to Islam, 20, 30, 110, 119,
     146
   to Judaism, 9, 47, 49, 79–80,
     107–111, 113, 116–119,
     133, 135, 139–140
   pressure for, 113–114

to Protestantism, 116
rejection of, 111–113
Council of Jewish Federations,
3, 12
counseling, 10, 27–28, 56
interfaith, 145
premarital, 31–32

D
discrimination, religious, 72,
130
dispensation, 5–6
Diwali, 36–37
Dunitz, Mimi, 62

E
Easter, 1–2, 36, 38, 42, 58, 65,
77, 78, 85, 86
education, religious, 4, 16–17,
34, 41–44, 49, 55, 57, 61,
67, 68, 94–102, 163
eids, 36, 83
Elliott, Father Mark, 7–8, 22–
23, 32, 38, 53, 54, 66
environment
culturally diverse, 18–20
religious, 15–16
ethnicity
differences in, 37, 47, 64,
121, 160
heritage of, 99, 128
Jewish, 59

F
faith, practice of, 37–41, 128–
129
family
Buddhist-Christian, 2, 20, 29,

47, 51, 66, 68, 146
Catholic-Jewish, vii, 16, 17–
18, 22, 23, 46, 49, 54–55,
58, 63–64, 67, 75–77, 90–
91, 95, 101, 111–112
Catholic-Orthodox, 2, 28–29
Catholic-Protestant, vii, 2,
12, 16, 19, 25, 29, 39, 48,
55, 91, 92, 101, 108, 155
Christian-Jewish, 19, 22, 28,
30, 48, 50, 59, 77, 111, 157
Christian-Muslim, vii, 2, 20,
29, 67, 82–83, 99
extended, 27, 66, 144
Hindu-Jewish, vii, 2, 24, 51–
52, 69, 78–79, 98, 113
Hindu-Sikh, 2
Jewish-Protestant, vii, 2, 9,
15, 17, 19, 22, 28, 29, 48,
51, 93, 103
Muslim-Protestant, 20, 30
Friedman, Felice, 56, 60, 145,
163
friends
attitude of, 86–88
religion of, 69–71, 130

G
Gerson, Rabbi Gary, 27
grandparents
as factor in religious identity,
52–53, 63–64
and holiday observance, 87–
88
Gray, the Reverend Donna, 8,
32, 38, 49, 54, 61, 116,
122, 141, 153
Greek Orthodox, 3, 7, 22, 32
Greenwood, Dru, 145

H

haircutting ceremony, 35
hajj, 36, 99
Hannigan, Frank, 3, 31–32,
    41–42, 61, 115, 141, 162
Hanukkah, 36, 69, 75–77, 78,
    79, 80, 81, 87, 140
Hart, Rabbi Stephen, 12, 27,
    39, 42, 79, 97–98, 102,
    118, 133, 139
High Holy Days (Holidays), 36,
    39, 78, 84–85, 100, 102
Hille, 28, 123
Hinduism, 11, 14, 18, 35, 41,
    43, 52, 66, 104
Hoge, Dean, 108
holidays, religious, 34, 75–89,
    155
home, keeping
    Buddhist, 40–41, 66, 68, 78,
        98, 100
    Catholic, 37–38, 67, 78, 87,
        101
    Christian Orthodox, 38
    Hindu, 41
    interfaith, 17–18
    Jewish, 27, 30–31, 39–40,
        42, 59, 68, 77–78, 80, 82,
        86, 90–91, 93–94, 109, 128
    Muslim, 40, 67
    Protestant, 38
house of worship, choosing,
    100–106

I

interdating, 14–15, 52, 131–
    134
intermarriage, attitudes toward
    in the Bible, 4

Buddhist, 11
Catholic, 3, 5–7, 31–32
Christian Orthodox, 3–4, 7–
    8
Hindu, 11
Jewish, 4, 9–11
Muslim, 11
Protestant, 8–9
intermarriage, religious policies
    on, viii, 4–13, 60–61
intermarriage, as threat to
    Judaism, 21–22, 27
Introduction to Judaism, 28,
    118, 145–146
Islam, 11, 29, 36, 40, 60

J

Jainism, 14, 104, 136
Jews By Choice, 109, 131
Judaism, 14, 35, 39–40, 42–43,
    70
    Conservative, 9–10, 39, 42,
        60, 103, 116–117
    Humanistic, 103–104
    Orthodox, 9, 23, 60, 116–117
    Reform, 4, 10, 12, 27, 39–40,
        42, 60, 97–98, 102, 103,
        116–118, 136, 139, 145

K

Kaiman, Rabbi Arnold, 27
kashruth (keeping kosher), 39,
    87, 117
Kovacs, David, 133
Kudan, Rabbi Harold, 105
Kurtz, Rabbi Vernon, 2, 10, 39,
    117, 140

L
Lawless, Richard, 91–92
Lent, 38, 39

M
Man Keung Ho, 3
marriage, officiating at, 8, 9,
    10–11, 23, 25–29
Marriage Encounter, 141
mass, 37, 101
Mayer, Egan, 108–109, 133
menorah, 40, 75–77, 79, 80, 81
mezuzah, 40
mikvah, immersion in, 117, 118

N
naming ceremony, 35

O
Outreach, 118, 133, 139, 142–
    145

P
parents, and intermarriage, 10,
    20–25
Passover, 1–2, 36, 68, 77, 78
    seder, 40, 85, 87, 113, 118,
    143
Place, Father Michael, 6, 37,
    115, 119, 161, 162
Protestantism, 35, 38–39

R
Raksha Badahn, 37
Ramadan, 36
relationship, interfaith, viii, 10,
    15–16
    building, 63–74
    religions, learning about other,

57–58, 153–154
religious identity, 3, 45–62
    changing, 121–137
    choosing, for children, 49–
    52, 157
    chosen by child, 56–57
    conflicts over, 155–156, 161
    confusion about, 48, 54, 126–
    127
    dual, 46, 50, 53–55, 63–64,
    75–77, 154, 159–160
    parent's own, 58–59
    and social environment, 129–
    137
    respect, 43, 48, 162–163
    rituals, religious, 28, 34–37
Rosenblum, Tema, 49, 60, 127,
    145, 160, 161
Rosh Hashanah, 36, 77, 84, 87
Russian Orthodox, 3, 85

S
sabbath, 33, 39–40, 117, 118,
    128
Scarlatta, Father Ron, 7, 162
Schwartz, Rabbi Gedalia Dov,
    9, 39, 116–117
Shahadah, 119
Sikhism, 14, 52, 66, 68, 104
Stepping Stones, 144
support group, 138–149
    Catholic-Jewish, 133, 140,
    141–142
    Catholic-Protestant, 141
    Islamic, 146

T
teenagers, interfaith, 121–137
Ten Commandments, 38, 43, 44

Thanksgiving, 38, 63

U
Upanayana, 35

V
value system, 42–44

Vatican Council II, 5, 7, 8, 114

W
wedding, planning, 25–26, 28–29

Y
Yom Kippur, 36, 77, 84